Mexican Cantina Cooking

Authentic Recipes to Capture the Flavours of Mexico

First published in the UK in 2007 by
Apple Press
Sheridan House
114 Western Road
Hove BN3 1DD
United Kingdom
www.apple-press.com

Editors
Josien Berkenvelder, Jessica Verbruggen,
Loes Verhoeven, Jean-Pierre Vincken

Managing Editor
Anda Schippers

Art Director
Mathieu Westerveld

Photography
Karin Anema, Remco Lassche, Désirée
Hanssen, Paula Mulder, Ger Reijntjes

Food
Monique van Esch

Styling
Rosanne Verstoppen

Assistant Editor
Josje Kets

Editor
Pieter Harts

Printer
Bookprint S.L.

Many thanks to
Brassa, Dille & Kamille, Ikea, Subba,
Verre Mediterranean home decorations,
Zus & Zo kitchen utensils and
Lucy Provoost

©Dutch Language edition Miller Books
e-mail: info@millerbooks.nl
www.millerbooks.nl

© Visconti

ISBN   978-1-84543-177-8

There is no other country where living takes place in the open air as much as in Mexico. In numerous cafés, such as the busy, popular cantinas, but especially at simple little stalls along the road and on markets, people live it up in an exuberant atmosphere. The wonderful aromas of the special herb and spice mixes of the Mexican kitchen tempt everyone out of their homes and encourage them to try numerous little snacks or more elaborate dishes.

The music of the Mariachi orchesteras, with song accompanied by guitar, violin and trumpet, make living outside even more attractive. In the background, the sounds of the country-like rancheras or the huapango (the "song of the tear") brings people together, while the rousing jarabe contributes to the party atmosphere. Especially when combined with a glass of tequila - pure or in a festive mixer, such as a Margarita - or with one of the fresh Mexican beers such as Corona or Carta Blanca. In addition, there are always big jugs of agua fresca within reach. These are cooled drinks made from pureed fruit, such as agua de tamarindo, or agua de Jamaica which is made from hibiscus flowers.

6

TASTY SNACKS

Antojitos are a favourite. This is a collective name for small bites eaten as a snack or as a starter in a restaurant. As this book will show you, the Mexican kitchen consists of so much more than endless variations on the *tortilla*, the thin, flat pancakes made of maize flour (*masa harina*). We can, however, quite confidently state that the antojitos, often with a tortilla as a base, are the most characteristic Mexican dishes. First of all, because they represent that real feeling of living al-fresco, but especially because maize (corn) is its main ingredient, and maize is one of the most important ingredients in the Mexican cuisine. It was grown by the Mayas, and later by the Aztecs, who mainly populated the middle part of Mexico. For centuries, tortillas have been made by flattening small balls of dough as much as possible and frying them on a hot griddle (*comal*). Many variations on the tortilla, basically the bread of the Mexicans, were created this way. For instance, the well-known *taco*: a folded, filled tortilla. Or the *enchilada*: where the tortilla is first dipped into a sauce, followed by shallow frying with lots of splattering, after which it is rolled up with a delicious filling. And how about *quesadillas*: parcels of folded tortillas, filled with cheese or something else, and then shallow or deep-fried or grilled.

The *burrito* is another story: it is actually also a tortilla, but made of wheat flour, which was only introduced in the sixteenth century by the Spanish. Especially in North Mexico, where maize wouldn't grow, wheat was an excellent replacement. Burritos made from wheat flour, however, do not have the characteristic, fresh taste of corn tortillas.

Masa harina, the basic ingredient of the tortilla, is also used to make *tamales*. These are steamed festive bites made of pastry, wrapped in a maize or banana leaf. Even *atole*, a milk-like drink or porridge, which may contain almonds or chocolate is made from corn.

Corn, beans and pumpkins (the flesh as well as the seeds) have been the staple ingredients of the Mexican Indian cuisine. However, the flavour of the dishes was and is especially determined by the large variety of chilli peppers. Chillies are not only hot, but each chilli has its own particular flavour.

Hot! CHILLIES IN MEXICO

- **POBLANO.** A large, triangular-shaped, green chilli with a purple bloom, not too hot. This pepper is always roasted and peeled, because the thick skin is quite tough. Poblanos are often stuffed with something nice (*chili rellenos*).
- **JALAPEÑO.** A green, slightly smaller chilli with a blunt tip. The flesh is medium hot to hot and is mainly used in salsas. Ripe jalapeños are red, less hot and slightly sweeter. Dried and smoked jalapeños are called *chipotles*.
- **SERRANO.** These small "mountain chillies" are often sold in their green version. Very hot and the chilli usually used for guacamole.
- **HABANERO.** The hottest of them all! The small habaneros can be red or yellowish and are shaped like a lantern. It can irritage the skin of your fingers, so imagine it on your tongue...
- **ANCHO.** This dried poblano is dark red and broad (*ancho* = broad) and has a somewhat fruity flavour. It is usually a bit hotter than the fresh version.
- **CASCABEL.** These dried round, chocolate brown or dark red peppers have loose seeds that rattle when you shake the chilli (*cascabel* = rattle). Not too hot and very suitable for salsas.
- **CHIPOTLE.** This is the name for dried and smoked jalapeños. They are very hot and add a smoky flavour to dishes. Therefore they are ideal for salsas or a sauce for barbecued meat or other meat dishes.

7

Inexperienced chilli eaters usually discover the really hot ones, with steam coming out of their ears, whereas the more experienced Mexicans make their decision based upon the flavour of the chilli. For instance, the hottest of all chillies, the *habanero*, has a flavour reminiscent of tropical fruit (which we won't taste, since it's chokingly hot!). This means this chilli goes well with dishes with fruit, tomatoes and salsas. The *poblano* chilli is less hot, and also known as *ancho* in its dried form. Poblano and ancho are the chillies most used for the *moles*. These are (often complicated) Mexican sauces (such as *guacamole,* the thick avocado sauce), made with anything nature has to offer: from spices, vegetables and seeds to chocolate - and, of course, a large dose of chillies.

OTHER SEASONINGS

Many seasonings were only introduced to the Mexican cuisine in later centuries, through the Spanish trade. Chocolate (with the Indian name *xocolatl*) has, however, an age-old history. Really, it was a thing of the gods, and only men were allowed to each chocolate. Mexican chocolate isn't sweet and is often flavoured with spices such as cinnamon or vanilla and nuts. Plain chocolate is one of the main ingredients of the mole poblano. According to tradition, nuns already made this dark, rich sauce in the seventeenth century.

The tomato, named *jitomate* by the aboriginal population, is a typical native ingredient of the Mexican cuisine. Although the tomato has certainly established itself in Western, and especially Mediterranean, cooking, you can tell from the Indian name where it originated. In Mexico, tomatoes are used in salsas, hearty moles and other stews. *Tomatillos* may look somewhat like tomatoes, and are often referred to as green tomatoes, even though they aren't.

MASA HARINA

Although we call the basic ingredient for tortillas maize flour, that is not what it really is! The Mexicans boil the corn kernels first in powdered lime. This makes it easy to remove the tough skin of the kernels. The thoroughly washed corn kernels are then ground to a moist and kneadable dough (*masa*). To make this dough easier to preserve, it is dried and ground to a fine powder called *masa harina*. By mixing this powder with warm water and kneading the mixture, corn dough is created, which can be used to make scrumptious tortillas.
Tamales are made with a slightly coarser corn dough, which is mixed with butter or lard. This gives the mixture its own specific flavour and makes it creamy, which is essential for these savoury or sweet party snacks.

Tomatillos are green, slightly tart berries surrounded by a thin membrane. The use of tomatillos in *salsa verde* gives this sauce its sharp, invigorating and fresh flavour. Alas, in Europe they are often only available in cans. Spanish tradesmen may have managed to distribute typical Mexican ingredients such as chillies, chocolate and tomatoes around the world, but they have also introduced new ingredients that have been completely absorbed by the native cuisines. Spices such as cloves, cinnamon and cumin, and fresh herbs such as thyme, oregano and coriander have become essential to the typical Mexican flavour! For instance, take *seviche,* raw fish "cooked" in lime juice, or imagine guacamole without coriander...

10

FOOD IN MEXICO

Mexico is a large country, with various climate zones, mountainous and coastal regions, deserts and jungles.

It therefore follows, that we cannot talk of "the" Mexican cuisine. Each region has its own specialities and uses the ingredients that are available locally. For example, in the North, it's not possible to grow corn, and people usually make wheat burritos, which they then characteristically use to wrap food cooked on the barbecue. In the coastal regions, fish dishes such as the *pescado a la veracruzana,* are served. While in the inland regions, the aromatic and typically spiced moles and stews, combined with corn tortillas and tacos, are on the menu. However, the times at which people eat are pretty much the

BEANS AND CHILLIES

If the tortilla is the Mexican's bread, then beans, *frijoles,* are the potato. Beans are presented in all sorts of dishes. Boiled beans to accompany the main meal, beans as part of stews, soups, sauces, or as a filling for tortillas. And let's not forget the *frijoles refritos,* pureed, boiled beans that are fried with herbs.

Beans can therefore be found in all shapes, sizes and colours at the Mexican markets, including black beans, often prepared with the herb goosefoot (*epazote*), which is one of the most well-known seasonings, and white beans or red kidney beans and *pinto* beans, with their distinctive pink colour and purple spots.

same throughout Mexico. The day usually starts simple, with coffee and a sweet roll. But if there is time, or otherwise later in the morning, a more elaborate breakfast (*desayuno*) follows, with fruit and fried eggs on a tortilla with chilli sauce, sometimes served with beans, a dish called *hueva rancheros*. The main meal of the day is lunch, *la comida,* which the Mexicans prefer to eat at home. It usually consists of several courses and is served from about 2pm. Firstly, people pull up a chair to enjoy a traditional bowl of soup. This is followed by a rice dish, a meat dish, often including beans, and tortillas and the meal is concluded with sweets.

La cena, the evening meal or dinner, is less elaborate and usually consists of lighter bites. People often use the evening to go out and enjoy smaller dishes in one of the numerous cafés. In *restaurantes*, food is a bit more elaborate, but eating snacks from little street vendors is a favourite: *comida callejera*. Last, but not least, Mexico is a country of festivals: nowhere in the world are as many festivals held as there are here. In addition to official holidays, each region has its own specific commemorative and other special days. And if that wasn't enough, everyone has his or her own saint's day in addition to his or her birthday. Festivals are celebrated in a noisy and happy atmosphere, with many appropriate snacks and drinks. In short:

Fiesta Mexicana!

12

Comida callejera

Empanadas Con Atún

Tuna Turnovers

20 thin rounds of empanada pastry: basic recipe (see box) • 1½ tbsp corn oil • 1 onion, chopped • 2 cans tuna (each about 225g/8oz) • 100ml/4fl oz/½ cup tomato sauce • 2 red peppers, deseeded and chopped • 2 tomatoes, skinned and chopped • 2 tbsp fresh parsley, chopped • salt and freshly ground black pepper • 2 hard-boiled eggs, shelled and chopped

EMPANADAS (RECETA BÁSICA)
(basic recipe)

For 10 empanadas: 200ml/7fl oz/¾ cup water • 1 tsp salt • 80g/3oz butter • 350g/12oz plain flour • 1 egg • oil for deep-frying

16

Heat the water with the salt and butter in a small pan, until the butter has melted. Pour the mixture into a mixing bowl, and add the flour. Stir until all the liquid has been absorbed. Add the egg, and stir thoroughly. Dust the worktop with flour, and place the pastry on it. Knead the pastry until it is soft and elastic and no longer sticky. Add more flour if necessary. Put the pastry back in the bowl, cover with a cloth and leave for 45 minutes. Divide the pastry into 12 equal pieces. Roll them out into thin rounds each about 10cm in diameter.

1 Heat the oil in a frying pan. Add the onion and fry until translucent.
2 Drain the tuna well, and mash finely. Combine the tuna, tomato sauce, peppers, tomatoes and parsley with the mixture in the pan. Add a little salt and pepper.
3 Leave to simmer for about 10 minutes until thickened. Take the pan off the heat and sprinkle with the egg.
4 Put a large tablespoonful of the tuna mixture in the middle of each round of pastry. Brush the edges with water, fold each round in half and use a fork to seal the edges. Repeat until you have 20 empanadas.
5 You can deep-fry the empanadas in hot oil until brown, or bake them in a fairly hot oven at 180°C/gas mark 4/350°F for about 25 minutes. When oven-baking, whisk 2 egg yolks together with a little water, and brush the empanadas with the mixture before putting them in the oven. Serve hot.

18

Empanadas con Carne de Vaca

Beef Turnovers

20 thin rounds of empanada pastry: see basic recipe (p. 16) • 1 litre/1¾ pint/4 cups beef stock • 500g/1¼lb lean stewing steak, cut into ½cm/¼in cubes • 1 medium onion, halved • 3 cloves garlic, peeled • 3 tbsp corn oil • 250g/9oz ripe tomatoes, roasted, skinned and finely chopped • 2 spring onions, finely chopped • 1-2 fresh Poblano chillies or 2-3 fresh green Lombok chillies, deseeded and chopped • salt • 2 tbsp fresh oregano, coarsely chopped

1 Heat the stock in a large pan. Add the meat and skim off the scum that floats to the surface in the first few minutes. Reduce the heat, until the stock bubbles slightly.
2 Cut one half of the onion into rings, and add to the pan, together with 1 clove of garlic. Add more water if the meat is not or no longer covered.
3 Leave the meat to simmer until it is cooked (about 1-2 hours). Remove the pan from the heat and leave to cool.
4 Remove the meat from the pan with a slotted spoon. Reserve 250ml/8fl oz/1 cup stock.
5 Finely chop the other half of the onion plus the 2 cloves of garlic. Heat the oil in a large, heavy-based frying pan and add the chopped onion and cooked meat as soon as the fat is hot. Stir-fry for 5-10 minutes over a medium heat, until the meat is brown.
6 Lower the heat, add the chopped garlic, tomatoes, spring onions and chillies and leave to simmer for another 4 minutes, until the tomatoes are soft.
7 Add the reserved stock, bring to the boil and leave to reduce for 10-15 minutes, until the liquid has almost completely evaporated. Season with salt and oregano.
8 Put a large tablespoonful of the meat mixture in the middle of each round of pastry. Brush the edges with water, fold each round in half and use a fork to seal the edges.
9 You can deep-fry the empanadas in hot oil until brown, or bake them in a fairly hot oven at 180ºC/gas mark 4/350ºF for about 25 minutes. When oven-baking, whisk 2 egg yolks together with a little water, and brush the empanadas with the mixture before putting them in the oven. Serve hot.

20

Empanadas con Carne de Cerdo y Almendras

Pork and Almond Turnovers

20 thin rounds of empanada pastry: see basic recipe (p. 16) • 1½ tbsp corn oil • 1 onion, chopped • 1 clove garlic, chopped • 500g/1¼lb lean pork, coarsely minced • ½ tsp black peppercorns, ground • 1 tsp ground cinnamon • 1 tsp ground cumin • 5 ripe tomatoes, roasted or blanched, skinned and puréed • 30g/1oz raisins • 4 tsp white wine vinegar • 20g/¾oz flaked almonds, toasted • salt

1 Heat the oil in a large frying pan, add the onion and fry over a medium heat until translucent. Add the garlic about 2 minutes before the onion is cooked.
2 Add the meat and fry until lightly browned and cooked, stirring regularly (pour any fat out of the pan).
3 Sprinkle the ground pepper, cinnamon and cumin over the meat, then add the puréed tomatoes, raisins and vinegar. Bring the mixture to the boil and leave to simmer and reduce to a thick mass.
4 Stir the almonds through the meat mixture and season with salt.
5 Put a large tablespoonful of the pork mixture in the middle of each round of pastry. Brush the edges with water, fold each round in half and use a fork to seal the edges.
6 You can deep-fry the empanadas in hot oil until brown, or bake them for 25 minutes in a fairly hot oven at 180ºC/gas mark 4/350°F. When oven-baking, whisk 2 egg yolks together with a little water, and brush the empanadas with the mixture before putting them in the oven. Serve hot.

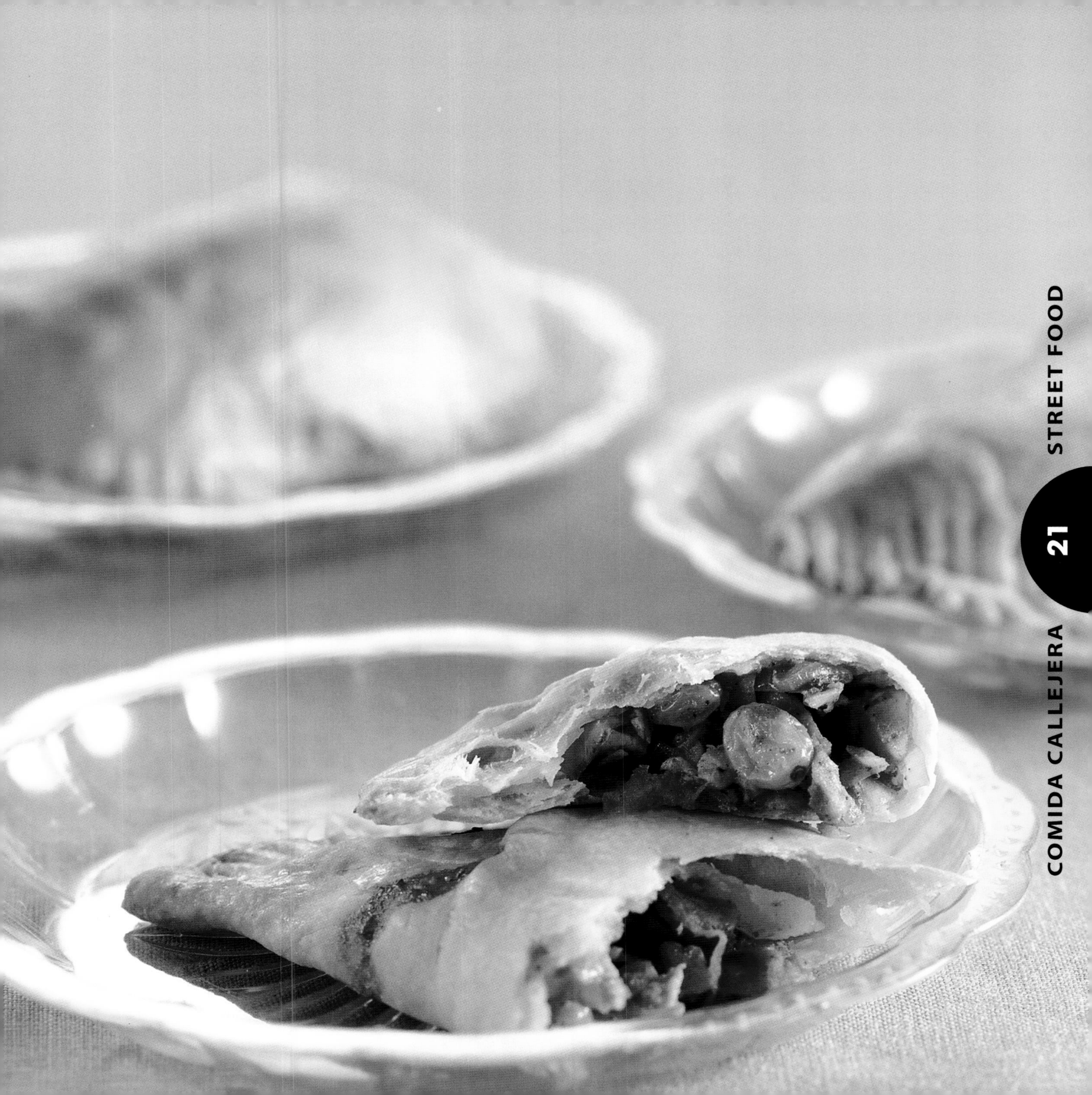

Empanadas con Queso

Cheese Turnovers

20 thin rounds of empanada pastry: see basic recipe (p. 16) • 150g/5oz waxy potatoes, peeled • salt • 1½ tbsp corn oil • 1 onion, thinly sliced • 1 clove garlic, chopped • 3 medium-sized fresh Poblano chillies, roasted, skinned and deseeded • 100g/4oz Queso Fresco, goat's cheese or feta, crumbled

CHEESE Although the country isn't especially known for its cheeses, Mexico does produce a variety. Cheese from Chihuahua *(Queso de Chihuahua)* is similar to English Cheddar, or a slightly matured Dutch Gouda. *Queso Fresco* is tangy and can easily be substituted with feta, ricotta or goat's cheese. *Queso Añejo or Seco*, an old, dry, crumbly cheese can best be compared to Parmesan or a nicely matured Manchego.

1 Boil the potatoes in a pan of lightly salted water until almost tender. Drain well, then cut them into cubes.
2 Heat the oil in a medium frying pan and fry the potato cubes, onion rings and garlic for 10-15 minutes over a medium heat, stirring occasionally, until the mixture is a nice golden brown.
3 Cut the flesh of the chillies into narrow strips. Stir the strips through the potato mixture and add salt to taste.
4 Take the pan off the heat, and stir the cheese through the potato mixture.
5 Put a large tablespoonful of the cheese mixture in the middle of each round of pastry. Brush the edges with water, fold each round in half and use a fork to seal the edges.
6 You can deep-fry the empanadas in hot oil until brown, or bake them in a hot oven at 180ºC/gas mark 4/350ºF, for about 25 minutes. When oven-baking, whisk 2 egg yolks together with a little water, and brush the empanadas with the mixture before putting them in the oven. Serve hot.

Tacos Blandos con Gambas y Aliño de Limón

*Soft Tacos with
Prawns and a Lime Dressing*

12 corn tortillas: see basic recipe (p. 122) • 300g/11oz large raw prawns (frozen), unpeeled • 1 lime, halved • ½ tsp black peppercorns, crushed • ¼ tsp whole allspice, crushed or coarsely ground • salt • 1 large red onion, cut into ½cm/¼in cubes • 1 ripe tomato, skinned, deseeded and cut into 1½cm/¾in cubes • 2 tbsp fresh coriander, finely chopped • juice of 1 lime • 6 tbsp corn oil • salt and freshly ground black pepper

24

REFRESHING Cilantro is the Mexican name for coriander. It is usually used for sprinkling over dishes, or it is added to a dish at the last moment. When it is cooked too long, the herb loses its lovely, refreshing taste. A word of warning: not everybody loves the distinctive taste of coriander. Therefore, use slightly less and allow people to add some more, if desired.

1 Defrost the prawns. Squeeze the juice out of the lime halves into a medium pan, pour in 500ml/17fl oz/2 cups water and add the squeezed lime halves, black pepper, allspice and salt.
2 Bring the water to the boil and leave to infuse on a low heat, with the lid on the pan, for about 10 minutes. Turn the heat up, add the prawns, and bring to the boil again. Take the pan off the heat when the prawns are cooked, then drain the prawns, discarding the cooking liquid and lime halves.
3 Peel the prawns, score the full length of their backs, and remove the dark intestinal tract. Cut the prawns into 1½cm/¾in pieces.
4 Mix the onion and tomato with the prawns, then add the coriander. Set aside.
5 Make a dressing by mixing together the lime juice, oil and a pinch of salt. Pour the dressing over the prawns and stir carefully and thoroughly to mix. Season the salad with salt and/or pepper, if necessary.
6 Meanwhile, steam the corn tortillas over a pan of boiling water or in a steamer. Place some prawn filling onto the centre of each tortilla and fold it twice. Serve immediately.

Fajitas con Tiras de Bife y Cebollas Fritas

Fajitas with Beef Strips and Fried Onions

12 corn tortillas: see basic recipe (p. 122) • 500g/1¼lb thin frying steaks • salt and freshly ground black pepper • 3 tbsp corn oil • 1 large onion, sliced • 2 large cloves garlic, finely chopped • 4 tbsp fresh coriander, coarsely chopped

26

FESTIVAL Cattle is mainly raised on the North Mexican grasslands and upland plains. There, the *charros*, Mexican cowboys, used to look after their herds on horseback. The art of horse-riding created the "charreria", a national sport, during which the *charros* have to undergo various tests of their skills in an arena. It is a sport, but also a festival during which traditional dress and mariachi music play an important part.

1 Pat the steaks dry with kitchen paper and season with salt and pepper. Heat the oil in a large, heavy-based frying pan and sear and brown the meat over a high heat (about 1-2 minutes per side).
2 Keep the steaks hot on a rack (with a plate underneath to catch the juices) in a preheated oven at the lowest setting. Lower the heat underneath the pan slightly.
3 Fry the onion in the remaining fat for about 10 minutes, stirring frequently, until it is a nice golden brown. Add the garlic and fry with the onion for about 2 minutes.
4 Cut the meat into strips at right angles, across the grain and keep warm. If necessary, season with salt.
5 Meanwhile, steam the corn tortillas over a pan of boiling water or in a steamer.
6 To serve, place the hot tortillas, meat, fried onion and garlic mixture and coriander in separate dishes. Everybody can then make their own filled fajitas. Top with tomato sauce, if desired.

Tacos Blandos con Setas en Salsa de Tomate

Soft Tacos with Mushrooms in Tomato Sauce

12 corn tortillas: see basic recipe (p. 122) • 250g/9oz mushrooms, brushed clean and coarsely sliced • 1 medium onion, chopped • 1 fresh Poblano chilli or 1 fresh green Lombok chilli, deseeded and finely chopped • 150ml/5fl oz/¾ cup chicken stock • juice of ½ lime • 1 tbsp corn oil • 2 ripe tomatoes, roasted, skinned and chopped • 2 cloves garlic, coarsely chopped • salt

CANNED Not available fresh in the UK, alas is the *huitlachoche*, a fungus that grows on corn. In Mexico, it is considered to be a real delicacy. You may very occasionally find this fungus in delis, in cans. It has a strong flavour, reminiscent of truffles. Seize the opportunity to buy it if you see it, because the scent as well as the taste are amazing.

1 Place the mushrooms, onion and chilli in a pan, add the stock, lime juice and oil and bring to the boil over a medium heat. Put a lid on the pan and leave to boil for a few minutes.
2 Remove the lid and leave the pan on the heat until all the liquid has evaporated and the mushrooms are beginning to fry in the fat.
3 Meanwhile, purée the tomatoes and garlic in a blender or food processor.
4 Once the mushrooms start to fry, pour the tomato purée into the pan, and leave to simmer and thicken for about 5 minutes, until the mixture has the consistency of a thick stew. Season the mushrooms with salt, then transfer the mixture to a bowl and leave to cool.
5 Steam the corn tortillas over a pan of boiling water or in a steamer. Place some mushroom filling onto the centre of each tortilla and fold it twice. Serve immediately.

Tacos Blandos con Calabacín y Carne de Cerdo

Soft Tacos with Courgettes and Pork

12 corn tortillas: see basic recipe (p. 122) • 4 small courgettes, cut into 1½cm/¾in cubes • salt • 2 tbsp corn oil • 500g/1¼lb lean pork, cut into 1cm/½in cubes • 1 small onion, thinly sliced • 3 cloves garlic, finely chopped • 1 ripe tomato, skinned and finely chopped • 1 large fresh Poblano chilli or 2 fresh green Turkish chillies, roasted, skinned, deseeded and cubed • sweetcorn kernels cut from 1 cob, or 200g/7oz frozen sweetcorn, defrosted • 100g/4oz fresh cheese, such as feta or goat's cheese, cut into 1cm/½in cubes

30

1 Put the courgette cubes in a sieve, sprinkle with salt and leave to drain for 30 minutes.
2 Heat the oil in a large frying pan. Add the meat cubes and sear and brown over a medium heat, stirring regularly. Using a slotted spoon, transfer the meat to a bowl.
3 Lower the heat, add the onion rings to the pan and fry for a few minutes, until golden brown. Add the garlic 1 minute before the onions are cooked, then add the tomato, and leave to simmer for 5 minutes, stirring occassionally.
4 Meanwhile, wash the courgette cubes under cold running water and pat dry with kitchen paper. Stir the courgette cubes, meat, chilli and sweetcorn through the onion mixture, then pour in 350ml/ 12fl oz/1½ cups water.
5 Bring the mixture to the boil and leave to simmer for about 30 minutes until the meat is cooked and the liquid has been almost completely absorbed. Add salt to taste.
6 Meanwhile steam the corn tortillas over a pan of boiling water or in a steamer. Place some pork filling in the centre of each tortilla and fold it twice. Serve immediately.

This dish is lovely served with guacamole (see box).

GUACAMOLE
Avocado Dip

2 large avocados • 1 tomato, skinned, deseeded and chopped • 1 spring onion, chopped • 2 fresh Serrano chillies, chopped • 1 tbsp fresh coriander, coarsely chopped • juice of ½ lime • salt

Mash the flesh of the avocados in a bowl and mix with the other ingredients. Add salt to taste.

Tacos Duros con Huevo Revuelto en Salsa Verde Picante

Hard Tacos with Scrambled Eggs in a Spicy Green Sauce

12 corn tortillas: see basic recipe (p. 122) • 4 large eggs • salt • 2½ tbsp corn oil, plus extra for frying • 60g/2oz white cheese, such as feta or goat's cheese, crumbled (plus extra for garnishing) • 2 small red onions, thinly sliced • 250g/9oz waxy potatoes, cubed • 2 large, fresh Poblano chillies or 2 fresh green Lombok chillies, roasted, skinned and cut into very narrow strips • 350ml/12fl oz/1½ cups salsa verde (see box)

TIP Mexicans love their eggs! Especially when having a late breakfast (*almuerzo*), which used to be eaten after an early breakfast of sweet rolls and coffee (*desayuno*). Nowadays, egg dishes such as *huevos revueltos*, also known as scrambled eggs, and *huevos rancheros* (fried egg with spicy tomato sauce) are available all day, often as a snack in the stalls along the street, and definitely nearly always in spicy combinations, even when it's still early!

32

SALSA VERDE
Green Sauce

250g/9oz canned tomatillos, drained • 1 small onion, finely chopped • 1 clove garlic, finely chopped • 2 or more fresh Serrano chillies, coarsely chopped • 1 tbsp fresh coriander, coarsely chopped • salt • a pinch of sugar

Mix all the ingredients in a blender or food processor, and leave to run for 2 minutes (no longer).

1 Beat the eggs with a pinch of salt in a bowl.
2 Heat a little of the oil in a large non-stick frying pan over a medium heat. As soon as the fat is hot, add the eggs. Stir the eggs every now and then to loosen them from the pan, until the eggs are scrambled but still moist and creamy. Spoon the scrambled eggs into a bowl, stir in the crumbled cheese and set the bowl aside. Clean the pan.
3 Put the frying pan back on the heat and heat the rest of the oil over a medium heat. Add half the onion rings and all the potato cubes and fry them for about 15 minutes, stirring regularly, until the potatoes have browned nicely. Add the strips of chilli and increase the heat slightly.
4 As soon as the vegetables start frying a bit more vigorously, add the salsa verde and leave the mixture to simmer and reduce for about 4-5 minutes, until the sauce thickens slightly and darkens. Continue to heat the sauce until it is reduced and thickened further. Stir in the scrambled eggs and cheese and leave to heat through for another minute or so.
5 Fill the corn tortillas with the egg mixture and roll them up. Fry them in a liberal amount of oil in a frying pan or deep-fat fryer until brown. Drain on kitchen paper. Garnish with the additional cheese and the rest of the red onion rings.

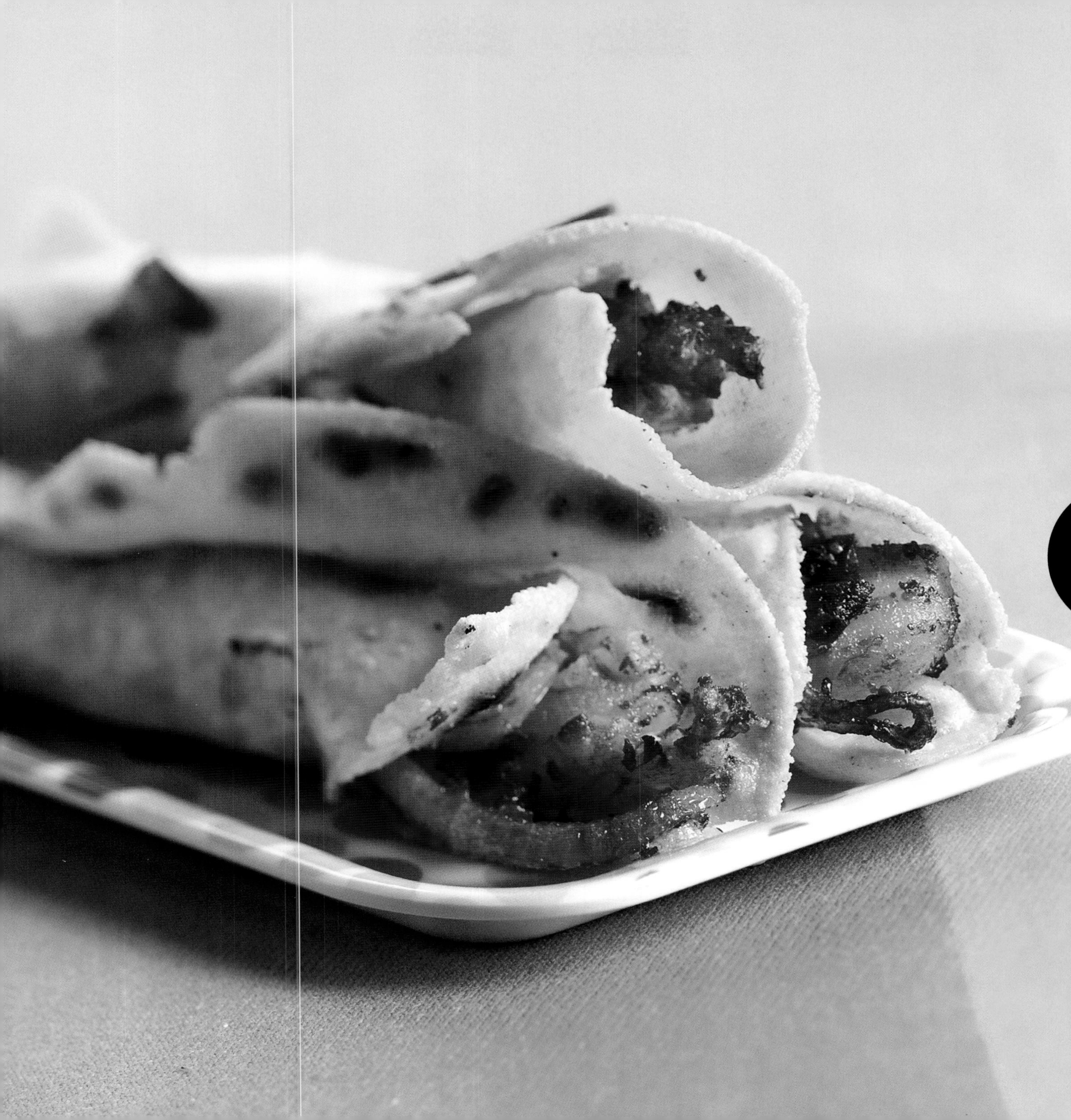

Tacos Duros con Pollo y Aguacete

Hard Tacos with Chicken and Avocado

12 corn tortillas: see basic recipe (p. 122) • 400g/14oz skinless bone-less chicken breasts • salt • 3 large waxy potatoes, halved • 4 tbsp white wine vinegar • 4 tbsp fresh oregano, coarsely chopped • 3 canned Chipotle chillies, deseeded and cut into thin strips • 1 small onion, finely chopped • 4 large lettuce leaves, cut into 1cm/½in strips • 1 ripe avocado, peeled, stoned and cut into small cubes • 4 tbsp corn oil, plus extra for frying • 2 tbsp flaked almonds, toasted

34

SALSA RANCHERA
Tomato Sauce

2 tbsp corn oil • 500g/1¼lb tomatoes, skinned, de-seeded and chopped • 1-2 fresh Jalapeño chillies, 2-3 fresh Serrano chillies or 3 fresh green Lombok chillies, de-seeded and chopped • salt • freshly ground black pepper

Heat the oil in a frying pan and add the toma-toes and chillies. Keep stirring until the toma-toes are reduced to a thick purée. Season with salt, pepper and, if neces-sary, sugar.

1 Poach the chicken in 500ml/17fl oz/2 cups salted boiling water in a pan for about 15 minutes, until tender. Remove the pan from the heat and leave the chicken to cool in the liquid.
2 Boil the potatoes in a pan of lightly salted water until just tender. Remove the pan from the heat and drain them. Peel the potatoes and cut into 1cm/½in pieces.
3 Tear the chicken into small pieces and mix with the potato cubes.
4 Mix 2 tablespoons of the chicken cooking liquid with the vinegar, oregano and a little salt and add to the potato mixture. Add the chillies and onion, mix well, then cover and put in the fridge for 45 minutes.
5 Add the lettuce and avocado cubes to the chicken mixture, sprinkle with the oil and mix lightly. Add the flaked almonds as the final touch.
6 Fill the corn tortillas with the chicken mixture and roll them up. Fry them in a liberal amount of oil in a frying pan or deep-fat fryer until brown. Drain on kitchen paper. Serve with tomato sauce (see box).

Tacos con Patatas y Chorizo

Soft Tacos with Potatoes and Chorizo

36

12 corn tortillas: see basic recipe (p. 122) • 500g/1¼lb waxy potatoes, halved • salt • 2 tbsp vegetable oil, plus extra for frying •
250g/9oz chorizo or merguez sausages, skin removed • 1 onion,
chopped • ½ bunch fresh oregano, coarsely chopped • 4 spring
onions, coarsely chopped

1 Cook the potatoes in a pan of lightly salted boiling water until
   almost tender, then drain. Peel them and cut into 2cm/¾in cubes.
   Set aside.
2 Heat the oil in a large frying pan and fry the chorizo for about
   10 minutes over a medium heat, until the meat is loose and crumbly.
   Remove the meat from the pan to a plate using a slotted spoon,
   ensuring the fat stays in the pan. Pour some of the fat out of the
   pan, leaving about 2 tablespoons in the pan.
3 Fry the potatoes and onion in the fat over a medium heat, stirring
   regularly, until the mixture is a nice golden brown (about
   15 minutes).
4 Add the fried chorizo, oregano and spring onions and heat through
   thoroughly, stirring occasionally. If necessary, season with salt.
5 Fill the corn tortillas with the potato mixture and roll them up. Fry
   them in a liberal amount of oil in a frying pan or deep-fat fryer until
   brown. Drain on kitchen paper. Serve hot.

38

Tacos con Tomate y Pollo

Soft Tacos with Tomatoes and Chicken

12 corn tortillas: see basic recipe (p. 122) • 500g/1¼lb skinless boneless chicken breasts • salt • 2 ripe tomatoes, roasted, skinned and coarsely chopped • ½ onion, coarsely chopped • 1 tsp ground cumin • ½ tsp aniseeds • 1 clove garlic, coarsely chopped • 2 tbsp corn oil, plus extra for frying • 5 tbsp crème fraîche or soured cream • 300ml chunky guacamole (see p. 30) • 1 tbsp Mexican or another fresh white cheese (such as feta or goat's cheese), crumbled

TIP Removing the skins from tomatoes is easy! Heat water in a pan until almost boiling, and use a sharp knife to make a cross in the top of the tomatoes. Stick each tomato on a fork, and dunk into the hot water for a few seconds. The skin will curl slightly where the cuts were made in the tomato. You can then peel it off easily.

1 Poach the chicken in a pan of lightly salted boiling water until tender. Remove the pan from the heat and leave the chicken to cool in the cooking liquid. Drain the chicken, then cut it into strips. Set aside.
2 Blend the tomatoes, onion, cumin, aniseeds and garlic in a blender or food processor until they form a smooth paste.
3 Heat 1 tablespoon oil in a medium frying pan and fry the tomato paste over a medium heat, stirring regularly, until it forms a thick sauce (about 4 minutes).
4 Stir the chicken through the tomato sauce and season with salt.
5 Fill the corn tortillas with the chicken mixture and roll them up. If necessary, secure with cocktail sticks. Fry them in a liberal amount of oil in a frying pan or deep-fat fryer until golden brown. Drain on kitchen paper.
6 Serve immediately with the crème fraîche, guacamole and cheese.

Buñuelos

Buñuelos

1 tsp salt • 1 tsp baking powder • 1 tsp ground aniseeds • 4 tbsp caster sugar • 750g/1¾lb plain flour • 2 large eggs • 250ml/8fl oz/ 1 cup milk • 60g/2oz unsalted butter, melted • oil, for deep-frying • 2 tbsp caster sugar, mixed with 1 tsp ground cinnamon • ½ tsp chilli powder

1 Mix the salt, baking powder, aniseed, sugar and flour in a bowl. Whisk the eggs with the milk in a separate bowl, then gradually incorporate it into the flour mixture. Stir in the melted butter, mixing well.
2 Place the dough on a lightly floured surface and knead until soft and elastic. Cover and leave to rest for 1 hour.
3 Divide the dough into 24 balls and, on a floured surface, flatten them or roll them out into rounds, each about 10cm/4in in diameter.
4 Heat the oil to 180°C/350°F in a deep-fat fryer and fry the dough rounds for 2 minutes on each side, until lightly browned.
5 Remove from the pan using a slotted spoon and leave to drain on kitchen paper. Dust with the cinnamon sugar and chilli powder.

Serve as a biscuit or as a dessert, with maple syrup.
Mexicans mainly eat buñuelos at Christmas, with a honey and aniseed sauce.

44

CINNAMON Cinnamon is not only an important flavouring for sweet dishes, it is also used in savoury stews. The Spanish imported cinnamon into Mexico, where it was initially used to give chocolate drinks some extra flavour. From then on, cinnamon - the dried bark of the *Cinnamomum Verum* - established itself as an ingredient in numerous dishes. Why not buy the soft, real cinnamon sticks instead of the powder, or the hard sticks of the cassia tree, and grind them yourself?

Molletes

Sweet Rolls

2½ tsp dried yeast granules • 1 tsp caster sugar • 125ml/4fl oz/ ½ cup lukewarm water • 250ml/8fl oz/1 cup full fat milk • 1 large egg, whisked • 30g/1oz butter, melted • 1 tsp aniseeds • 1 tsp salt • 60g/ 2oz granulated sugar • 750g/1¾lb plain flour, sifted • melted butter, for brushing • soft brown sugar, sifted • 2 tbsp ground cinnamon

WEEKEND BREAKFAST

Molletes or sweet rolls, sell like hot cakes at the baker's *(panaderías)*. When there isn't enough time, or it's too early to have a big breakfast with eggs, which basically applies to anyone with a standard job, the day in Mexico starts with a sweet roll. Here, they're delicious rolls to add to our weekend breakfast. The temptation is irre-sistible when you smell the delicious aromas wafting from the oven!

1 Mix together the yeast, 1 tsp caster sugar and water in a small bowl. Leave in a warm place for about 15 minutes or until a frothy head develops.
2 In a large bowl, mix together the milk, egg and melted butter. Stir in the aniseeds, salt and granulated sugar. Add the yeast mixture and mix well.
3 Slowly incorporate the flour to make a soft dough. Knead gently until smooth and elastic. Cover and leave to rest in a warm, draught-free place, until the dough has doubled in size.
4 Place the dough on a floured surface and divide into 24 equal pieces. Knead the dough into little balls and place on a greased baking tray. Cover loosely and leave to rise in a warm, draught-free place for another hour or so, or until they have doubled in size. Preheat the oven to 200ºC/gas mark 6/400ºF.
5 Brush the rolls with melted butter and sprinkle them with brown sugar and cinnamon. Bake in the oven for 15 minutes, until golden brown. Serve warm.

La Comida

Frijoles con Tocino, Guindillas Picantes Tostadas y Culantro Fresco

Beans with Bacon, Roasted Chillies and Fresh Coriander

250g/9oz (light-coloured) dried beans • 60g/2oz pork, not too lean, cut into 1cm/½in cubes • 4 thick slices back bacon or streaky bacon, cut into strips • 1 medium onion, finely chopped • 1 large, fresh Poblano chilli, roasted, deseeded, skinned and chopped • 3 small ripe tomatoes, grilled or blanched, skinned and cut into pieces • 1 tsp salt • 4 tbsp fresh coriander leaves, chopped

52

CLAY Mexicans used to cook their beans in an *olla*. These large ceramic pots are narrower at the top and are often glazed in bright colours. During cooking, the clay gives the dish a characteristic additional flavour. Although most people use normal pans nowadays, purists think the flavour of the clay is vital.

1 Boil the beans in a pan of boiling water for 1-2 minutes, then take the pan off the heat and leave for 1 hour.
2 Drain the beans, return them to the pan and add 2 litres/3½ pints cold water to the pan. Add the pork and slowly bring the mixture to the boil. Partially cover the pan with a lid and boil the beans for 1-2 hours until tender, stirring occasionally.
3 Heat a medium frying pan over a fairly low heat and fry the bacon strips until crispy. Remove the strips with a slotted spoon and set aside. Pour most of the fat out of the pan, leaving 2 tablespoons in the pan. Fry the onion and chilli in the fat, stirring occasionally, until the onion is a nice golden brown. Add the tomatoes and simmer gently until all the liquid has evaporated.
4 Stir the tomato mixture and bacon through the beans and season with salt. Leave the beans to simmer gently for another 20 minutes, so the flavours can infuse. If the pan still contains a fair amount of liquid, turn up the heat and let the sauce reduce and thicken for a few minutes.
5 Add the coriander to the beans just before serving.

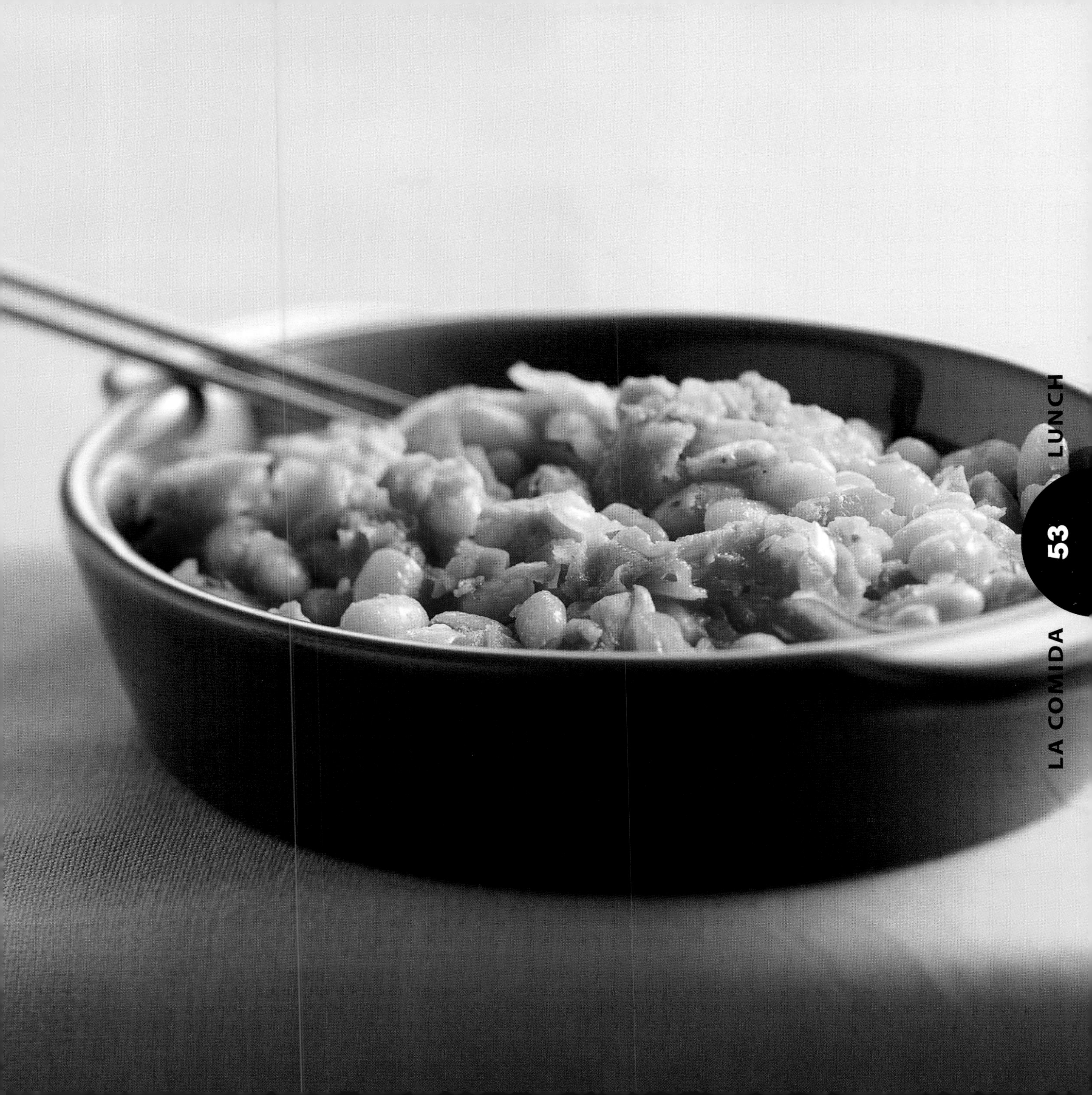

Arroz Verde con Guindillas Picantes y Guisantes

Green Rice with Chilli Peppers and Peas

½ medium onion, chopped • 1 stick celery, chopped • 6 sprigs fresh coriander • 6 sprigs fresh flat-leaf parsley • 2 fresh Poblano chillies, roasted, skinned, deseeded and chopped into pieces • 1 large clove garlic, sliced • 150ml/5fl oz/¾ cup vegetable stock • 1 tsp salt • 100g/4oz shelled peas, fresh or frozen • 1½ tbsp corn oil • 200g/7oz Arborio rice

1 Put the onion, celery, coriander, parsley, chillies and garlic in a small saucepan. Add 300ml/½ pint/1¼ cup water, put a lid on the pan and bring the water to the boil over a medium-high heat.
2 Boil the mixture for about 10 minutes, until the onion and celery pieces are soft. Take the pan off the heat and leave the contents to cool until lukewarm.
3 Purée the pan's contents (including liquid) in a blender or food processor, then pour the purée back into the pan and add the stock. Add salt to taste.
4 Cook the peas in a separate pan of lightly salted, boiling water until *al dente*, then rinse them with cold water and leave to drain (frozen peas only need to be defrosted). Keep warm.
5 Put the oil and rice in a separate pan. Heat the mixture over a medium-high heat, stirring constantly, until the rice grains become transparent (after about 7 minutes). Meanwhile, bring the stock mixture to the boil.
6 Pour the stock into the rice, stir well, then cover and leave the rice to simmer over a fairly low heat for 15 minutes. Take the pan off the heat, then leave it to sit, with the lid on, for 5-10 minutes.
7 Loosen the rice grains with a fork and mix in the peas. Serve immediately.

For red rice, add 200g/7oz skinned, chopped fresh tomato pieces to the rice. Fry the tomatoes for a few minutes and then add the stock.

54

HOT? The spiciness of the chilli is indicated on a scale from 1 to 10. Medium hot chillies, such as the Poblano, score below 5, but don't think that those horribly hot Habaneros, with a score of 10, are twice as hot as a chilli with a score of 5, because they're 75 times as hot! The spiciness of a chilli depends on the amount of *capsaicin* it contains.

Budín de Arroz

Rice Pudding

200g/7oz raisins • 100ml/4fl oz/½ cup tequila • 125g/4½oz short-grain pudding rice • 1 piece lime zest • pinch of salt • 1 cinnamon stick • 1 litre/1¾ pint/4 cups full fat milk • about 100g/4oz caster sugar • 2 large egg yolks, whisked • 50g/2oz pistachio nuts, chopped • toasted flaked almonds, to decorate

LATE SNACK Where we live, the chippies and the kebab shops do good business after the pubs close, but in Mexico, people go and get themselves a tub of rice pudding *(arroz con leche)*. The pub-crawlers saunter home while eating, or eat the dessert at home. However, rice pudding is usually served as a dessert during the big afternoon meal.

1 Soak the raisins in the tequila in a bowl for 10 minutes.
2 Put the rice in a heavy-based saucepan, together with the lime zest, salt, cinnamon stick and 750ml/1¼ pint/3 cups milk. Bring to the boil, stirring continuously, then turn the heat down and cover the pan.
3 Simmer gently for 30-40 minutes or until the rice is tender and most of the liquid has been absorbed, stirring occassionally. If required, add the rest of the milk.
4 Remove and discard the lime zest and cinnamon stick. Add the sugar to the rice mixture (do not add all the sugar in one go, add it to taste).
5 Stir the egg yolks, pistachio nuts and soaked raisins into the rice, then leave the mixture to simmer for a few more minutes.
6 Spoon the pudding into serving dishes and sprinkle with almonds. Eat the rice pudding at room temperature.

Crema de Coco con Almendras Tostadas

Coconut Crème with Toasted Almonds

125ml/4fl oz/½ cup coconut milk • 100g/4oz dried coconut flakes • 100g/4oz caster sugar • 6 large egg yolks • 2 tbsp milk • 20g/¾oz unsalted butter • 30g/1oz flaked almonds, toasted

1 Bring the coconut milk, coconut flakes and sugar to the boil in a heavy-based pan. Lower the heat and keep stirring until the coconut is translucent and most of the liquid has evaporated (20-30 minutes). Take the pan off the heat.
2 Whisk the egg yolks with the milk in a bowl, add a couple of spoonfuls of the hot coconut crème while stirring continuously, then pour the mixture into the pan with the rest of the coconut crème.
3 Put the pan over a low heat and cook gently, stirring continuously, until the crème has thickened (about 10 minutes).
4 Spoon the coconut crème into one large shallow oven-proof dish or divide it between 4 individual dishes and dot with the butter.
5 Put the dish under a preheated hot grill for 1-2 minutes, until the top is lightly browned. Sprinkle with the toasted almonds and serve immediately.

TIP On a day trip? This Coconut Crème is great for a picnic.

58

Flan

Crème Caramel

750ml/1¼ pint/3 cups milk • 1 vanilla pod, split open lengthways • 2 eggs • 6 egg yolks • 200g/7oz caster sugar • For the caramel: 10 tbsp granulated sugar • 5 tbsp water

1 Preheat the oven to 180°C/gas mark 4/350°F.
2 For the caramel, gently heat the sugar with the water in a heavy-based pan. As soon as the sugar gets a bit of colour, pour it into the prepared moulds. Tip the moulds (10cm/4in in diameter) so the sides are covered in caramel.
3 Pour the milk into a separate pan, add the vanilla pod and heat gently for 15 minutes to allow the flavours to infuse. Remove the pan from the heat and leave to cool for a little while.
4 Whisk the eggs, yolks and sugar together in a bowl. Gradually add the milk, stirring continuously. Strain the mixture through a sieve and pour it into the caramel moulds.
5 Put the moulds into a deep oven-proof dish. Fill the dish with boiling water up to two-thirds of the height of the moulds. Put 2 or 3 eggshells into the boiling water, so it does not splash into the moulds. Put the dish in the oven.
6 Check whether the flans are ready after 50 minutes. Prick the centre of a flan with a skewer: the skewer should be clean when it comes out. Remove the flans from the oven and leave to cool.
7 To serve, turn the flans out onto small serving plates. If necessary, briefly dip the base of the moulds in hot water, to loosen the flans and make them easier to turn out.

09

PX Why not combine a piece of flan with a glass of *Pedro Ximénez* (PX), a dark, sweet sherry. It isn't Mexican, but it is from a Spanish-speaking area, and it truly is a perfect combination.

Sopa de Maíz con Guindillas

Corn Soup with Chillies

300g/11oz sweetcorn kernels • 1 clove garlic, chopped • 1 onion, chopped • 90g/3½oz butter • 1 tsp ground cumin • 1 litre/1¾ pint/ 4 cups chicken stock (see box) • salt • 250g/9oz crème fraîche • 50g/2oz feta cheese, cut into cubes • 2 fresh Poblano chillies or 4-6 fresh green Lombok chillies, deseeded and coarsely chopped

CALDO DE POLLO (RECETA BÁSICA)
Chicken Stock (basic recipe)

1 oven-ready chicken, weighing about 1.5kg/ 3¼lb, cut into pieces • 2½ litres/4½ pints water • 1 small onion, quartered • 2 cloves garlic • 1 large carrot, sliced • 1 tbsp salt • 10 black peppercorns • 1 tbsp fresh parsley, chopped • 1 leek, sliced

62

1 Put the chicken in a pan with the water, onion and garlic.
2 Bring the mixture to the boil, removing any scum that floats to the surface.
3 When scum no longer floats up, add the remaining ingredients and leave to simmer for 2 hours.
4 Strain the stock through a sieve or colander and use immediately or leave to cool and chill until ready to use.

1 Purée the sweetcorn, garlic and onion in a blender or food processor. Set aside.
2 Heat the butter in a pan until melted, then add the sweetcorn purée and cumin and leave to simmer gently for 5 minutes, stirring occasionally.
3 Add the chicken stock, taste, and add salt if required. Leave to simmer for another 10 minutes.
4 Add the crème fraîche and leave to simmer again briefly. Remove the pan from the heat and pass the soup through a sieve into a clean pan. Reheat the soup gently until hot.
5 To serve, put 1 tablespoon cheese and about 2 teaspoons chillies in each serving bowl. Pour the soup on top and serve immediately.

Sopa de Ajo

Garlic Soup

25 cloves garlic, cut in half (see box) • 30g/1oz butter • 1 litre/ 1¾ pint/4 cups chicken stock: see recipe (p. 62) • salt and freshly ground black pepper to taste • pinch of freshly grated nutmeg • 2 egg yolks • 100ml/4fl oz/½ cup double cream

1 Sauté the garlic in the butter in a pan, ensuring they don't brown.
2 When the cloves are soft, add the stock, then leave the soup to simmer over a low heat for about 20 minutes.
3 Purée the soup with a hand-held blender and season with salt, pepper and nutmeg.
4 Mix the egg yolks with the cream in a bowl, then add a cup of soup. Stir well and add the mixture to the soup in the pan. Put the soup back onto the heat and heat gently, stirring continuously, until the soup is hot, but ensuring that it doesn't boil.
5 Foam the soup with a hand-held blender before serving. Pour the soup into warmed soup bowls and serve immediately.

64

GARLIC Don't worry about the large quantity of garlic used in this recipe. The longer the garlic is cooked, the softer and sweeter its flavour becomes.

Sopa de Tortilla

Tortilla Soup

3 cloves garlic • 1 onion, sliced • 2 tbsp corn oil • 3 ripe tomatoes, roasted and skinned (keep the juice) • 1 litre/1¾ pint/4 cups chicken stock: see recipe (p. 62) • 2 tbsp fresh parsley, coarsely chopped • salt and freshly ground black pepper • 6 soft flour tortillas, a few days old • oil, for deep-frying • 2 dried chillies (*Chiles Pasillas*), deseeded, membranes removed, cut into rings • 1 avocado, peeled, stoned and cut into strips • 200g/7oz feta cheese, cubed • 125ml/4fl oz/½ cup crème fraîche • 1 lime, cut into segments

1 Sauté the garlic and onion in 1 tablespoon oil in a pan until softened. Purée them in a blender or food processor, together with the tomatoes. If the purée is too dry, add a little chicken stock (no more than 50ml/2fl oz/¼ cup).
2 Heat the remaining oil in a large pan, add the purée and fry over a high heat. Bring to the boil and leave to boil for about 2 minutes. Lower the heat and cook the purée, stirring continuously, until it has reduced and changed colour (about 5 minutes).
3 Add the rest of the stock, together with the parsley. Bring back to the boil and add salt and pepper to taste, then leave to simmer over a low heat.
4 Cut the tortillas into small strips. Heat about 1cm/½in oil in a small, heavy-based pan and deep-fry the tortilla pieces for about 3 minutes, until golden brown. Drain the strips on kitchen paper.
5 Deep-fry the chillies in the hot oil too, for about 1 minute. Drain and set aside.
6 Put some serving bowls out and spoon the soup into them. Garnish each bowl with some chillies, deep-fried tortilla strips and avocado. Sprinkle the cheese on top. Serve the crème fraîche, lime segments and the rest of the chillies and avocado separately, in bowls alongside.

NO LUNCH WITHOUT SOUP Soup is a standard part of a big Mexican lunch. Especially in restaurants, people will find it odd if you start *La Comida* without soup. The *sopa de tortilla* is the most popular soup in Mexico, and has lots of regional variations.

Sopa con Bolitas de Gambas

Soup with Prawn Balls

For the prawn balls: 250g/9oz large raw prawns, peeled • 1 shal-
lot, finely chopped • ½ tomato, deseeded and cut into small
cubes • 1 large egg yolk • 2 tbsp plain flour • ½ tsp salt •
For the soup: 1 tbsp corn oil • 1 small onion, thinly sliced •
1 medium fresh Poblano chilli or 1-2 fresh green Lombok chillies, roasted, skinned, deseeded and cut into strips of about
2½cm/1in • 1 tomato, roasted, skinned and chopped • 1 litre/1¾
pint/4 cups fish stock • 1 tsp salt • 2 tbsp fresh coriander, coarsely
chopped • 1-2 limes, cut into segments

68

TIP In Mexico, sopa isn't always the soup we know. *Sopa agua-das* are the "wet" soups, but *sopas secas* are the second course on the menu, which are often rice or pasta dishes. The story goes that, when these ingredients were introduced, there was some confusion because both rice and pasta are boiled in a pan of water. It maybe that, because of the wet start of their preparation, these dishes are now called sopa.

1   For the prawn balls, use a large, heavy knife to chop the prawns into a coarse purée.
2   Put the prawn mixture in a bowl, add the other ingredients for the prawn balls and mix carefully. Cover and refrigerate.
3   For the soup, heat the oil in a large pan, add the onion and sauté over a medium heat until golden brown and transparent.
4   Add the chilli and tomato and fry for about 3-4 minutes. Pour in the stock, stirring continuously. Bring to the boil, then cover and leave to simmer for 15 minutes. Taste the soup and season with salt.
5   Meanwhile, shape the chilled prawn mixture into small balls. Put the balls into the soup and simmer gently for 5-8 minutes.
6   Spoon the soup into bowls and garnish with coriander. Serve the lime segments separately.

Pavo con Mole Rojo

Turkey with Red Mole

100g/4oz dried chillies, chopped • 1 tomato, roasted and skinned • 50g/2oz Mexican chocolate (or plain chocolate) or 2 tbsp unsweetened cocoa powder • ½ tsp aniseeds • 1 tsp ground cinnamon • 10 black peppercorns, crushed • 2 onions, chopped • 1 clove garlic, crushed • 2 tbsp raisins • 1 (old) soft tortilla, cut into strips • oil, for frying • 1 litre/1¾ pint/4 cups chicken stock: see recipe (p. 62) • 1 medium-sized oven-ready turkey, cut into portions • 100g/4oz flaked almonds, toasted • salt • 2 tbsp sesame seeds, toasted

1   Put the chillies in a bowl, pour over enough hot water to cover and leave to soak for 1 hour.
2   Mix the tomatoes, chocolate or cocoa powder, aniseeds, cinnamon and crushed peppercorns in a separate bowl. Set aside.
3   Fry the onion, garlic, raisins and tortilla in a little oil in a pan, for a few minutes, then add to the tomato mixture.
4   Stir the tomato mixture thoroughly. Put half of the tomato mixture in a blender or food processor, add 100ml/4fl oz/½ cup stock and blend to form a purée. If necessary, add a little extra stock.
5   Add this purée to the reserved half of the tomato mixture.
6   Drain the chillies, then purée them with a few tablespoons of stock. Set aside.
7   Fry the turkey portions in a little oil in a pan for 5 minutes, then remove them from the pan. Pour the excess fat from the pan.
8   Fry the chilli paste in the same pan, until it turns darker, then add the tomato mixture and almonds and leave to simmer for a few minutes. Thin the sauce with 600ml/1 pint/2½ cups stock. Season with salt.
9   Add the turkey to the pan and put the lid on. Simmer the turkey for 30 minutes or until cooked.
10 Garnish the dish with toasted sesame seeds and serve immediately.

70

SAUCE DISHES Moles, the chunky and complex Mexican sauces are really all-in-one dishes. The ceramic dishes in which they are prepared are called *cazuelas*. In the simple *fondas* (eateries) on markets there will always be a *cazuela*, simmering away with the favourite mole.

Muslo de Cordero Aobado del Horno

Marinaded Roast Leg of Lamb

2.5kg/5½lb leg of lamb • 100g/4oz dried Guajillos or Cascabel chillies, stalks, seeds and membranes removed • 6 cloves garlic, unpeeled • ¼ tsp cumin seeds, finely crushed • ½ tsp black peppercorns, crushed • 1 tsp salt • 3 tbsp white wine vinegar • 2 tsp caster sugar • 3 small ripe tomatoes, roasted and skinned • 1 tsp fresh oregano, chopped • 2 sprigs of fresh thyme • 1 cinnamon stick • 1 red onion, finely chopped • 2 tbsp fresh coriander, coarsely chopped • 2 limes, cut into segments

1. Cut off as much fat as possible from the lamb. Place the leg in a large non-metallic dish. Set aside.
2. Heat a griddle over a medium heat. Tear the chillies into flat pieces and put them on the griddle until they crackle and change colour. Turn them around and roast them on the other side. Remove them into a bowl, pour over some boiling water and leave to soak for 30 minutes.
3. Roast the garlic cloves on the griddle for 15 minutes, until the skin is blackened all over. Remove and leave to cool, then peel the cloves.
4. Drain the chillies and put them in a blender or food processor. Add the garlic, cumin, pepper, salt, vinegar and 175ml/6 fl oz/¾ cup water. Blend to form a smooth purée. Sieve the purée and put 125ml /4fl oz/½ cup in a bowl. Stir through the sugar and set aside.
5. Brush the meat with the rest of the purée, cover and put in the fridge for at least 4 hours.
6. Preheat the oven to 180ºC/gasmark 4/350ºF. Put a rack in a large roasting tin. Pour in 75ml/3fl oz/¼ cup water. Place the leg of lamb on the rack and cover the tin with foil. Put the lamb in the oven and "steam roast" the meat for 3 hours.
7. Remove the meat from the tin. Strain the liquid into a measuring jug. Spoon off the layer of fat and top the liquid up with water to measure 1 litre/1¾ pint/4 cups. Pour into a saucepan.
8. Purée the tomatoes in a blender or food processor and add to the liquid. Add the oregano, thyme and cinnamon stick, bring to the boil, then cover and simmer gently for 20 minutes. Add salt to taste.
9. Cut the meat from the bone, in large pieces. Put the meat onto a baking tray and brush all over with the reserved chilli purée. Bake in a hot oven at 220ºC/gas mark 7/425ºF for 10 minutes, until the meat is piping hot.
10. Mix the onion with the coriander. Serve the meat on a warmed serving dish and serve the tomato sauce, onion with coriander and the lime segments separately.

Mole Verde con Semilla de Calabaza con Pollo

Green Pumpkin Seed Mole with Chicken

4 skinless boneless chicken breasts • 1 onion, cut into quarters • salt • For the sauce: 120g/4oz pumpkin seeds, toasted • 350g/12oz tomatillos (canned), drained • 3 fresh Serrano chillies or 2 fresh Jalapeño chillies or 2 fresh Lombok chillies, deseeded and finely chopped • 5 large Romaine lettuce leaves • ½ onion, coarsely chopped • 3 cloves garlic, coarsely chopped • ½ tsp ground cumin • 6 black peppercorns, crushed • ½ tsp ground cinnamon • 1 clove • 1½ tbsp corn oil • ½ tsp salt • fresh parsley, chopped, for garnishing

1 Poach the chicken breasts in 1½ litres/2½ pints water in a pan with the onion quarters and salt, until the chicken is just tender. Remove the pan from the heat and leave the chicken to cool in the stock. Once cool, remove the chicken from the pan using a slotted spoon and set aside. Strain the stock into a jug and skim off the fat. Set aside and keep warm.
2 Finely grind the pumpkin seeds in a blender or food processor, together with 200ml/7fl oz/¾ cup of the chicken stock.
3 Mash the tomatillos finely with the green chillies in a bowl.
4 Tear the lettuce leaves and put the pieces into a blender or food processor, together with the chopped onion, garlic, cumin, pepper, cinnamon and clove. Blend to form a smooth purée.
5 Heat the oil in a pan, add the pumpkin seed mixture and fry until it thickens. Add the tomatillo purée and simmer, stirring continuously for a few minutes. Add 500ml/17fl oz/2 cups chicken stock, bring to the boil, then turn down the heat and leave to simmer gently for 30 minutes. Season the sauce with salt, and, if necessary, dilute it with a little extra stock.
6 Add the chicken breasts to the sauce and heat gently until piping hot. Place them on a warmed serving dish and spoon the sauce over them. Garnish with fresh parsley and serve immediately.

THICK OR THIN? Seeds, such as the pumpkin seeds in this recipe, are not only used for their flavour: ground seeds can also be used to thicken sauces or stews. Because dishes often get too thick during heating, it is usual to keep some stock behind to make them thinner.

Pescado en Salsa de Almendra y Culantro

Fish in Almond and Coriander Sauce

1kg/2¼lb fish fillets from a firm, non-oily white fish (such as hake or pollack) • 500ml/17fl oz/2 cups fish stock (see recipe below) • 3 tbsp corn oil • 1 clove garlic, peeled • 1 slice white bread • 4 tbsp flaked almonds • 2 fresh Serrano chillies or 1 fresh Jalapeño chilli, deseeded and finely chopped • 1 bunch fresh coriander • For the stock: 1 carrot, chopped • 1 onion, chopped • 1 leek, chopped • a little corn oil • 100ml/4fl oz/½ cup white wine • 1 bay leaf • 5 black peppercorns, crushed • 3 sprigs fresh thyme • 1 tsp salt • 1 litre/1¾ pint/4 cups water

80

MOIST FISH As the recipe states already: don't overcook the fish! Although the fish may be slightly translucent in the middle, which is something some people don't like, this is the right way to serve fish. Fish that is cooked too long loses too much moisture and becomes dry and loses flavour.

1 Make the stock by sautéing the carrot, onion and leek in a little oil in a pan. Add the wine, bay leaf, peppercorns, thyme, salt and water. Bring to the boil, then lower the heat, cover and leave to simmer gently for 20 minutes. Strain the stock into a jug.
2 Place the fish fillets in a large frying pan and pour the stock over. Bring gently to the boil over a medium heat and leave to simmer until the fish is no longer transparent. This will take about 5 minutes. Don't overcook the fish!
3 Remove the fish from the pan using a fish slice and leave to rest on a warm plate. Pour the stock into a jug. Set aside.
4 Heat the oil in a small frying pan and fry the garlic and bread over a medium heat until the bread is golden brown on both sides. Remove the garlic and cut the bread into pieces.
5 In a blender or food processor, process the bread with 2 tablespoons almonds, the chillies and coriander to form a paste. Dilute the paste with the reserved stock to make a sauce. Heat this sauce in a pan, then pour it over the fish. Garnish with the rest of the almonds and serve immediately.

Salmonete Sazonado

Spiced Mullet

6 dried chillies • 1 red mullet (about 300g/11oz), cleaned • plain flour, for dusting • salt • 4 tbsp corn oil • 1 onion, finely chopped • 2 cloves garlic, chopped • 1 bunch fresh coriander or parsley, coarsely chopped • 5 ripe tomatoes, skinned and chopped • ¼ tsp ground cumin • 2 tbsp fresh oregano, coarsely chopped

1 Roast the chillies in a dry frying pan for a few minutes, turning once. When they are done, remove them from the pan, remove the stalks and shake them to remove the seeds.
2 Tear the chillies into pieces, put them in a dish, and add enough boiling water to just cover them. Leave to soak for about 30 minutes, then drain and purée in a blender or food processor to make a paste. Set aside.
3 Dust the fish with flour and salt. Heat some oil in a large frying pan and fry the fish on both sides, until golden brown. Place the fish in an oven proof dish and leave to rest. Preheat the oven to 180°C/gas mark 4/350°F.
4 Fry the onion and garlic in the remaining oil in the pan until soft. Add the chilli purée, coriander, tomatoes, cumin and oregano and add some salt. Heat for about 5 minutes over a medium heat, stirring occasionally.
5 Pour the sauce over the fish, then bake it in the oven for about 30 minutes or until cooked. Serve immediately.

THUNDER AND LIGHT-NING The area around the gulf coast where this dish originates is the location where the Spanish landed in the sixteenth century. They must have boggled at, for instance, cities like El Tajín with its pyramids, and also its residential area, which was pretty modern for its time. The city is dedicated to the god of thunder and lightning, *Dios Tajín*.

Pescado con Tomates, Alcaparras y Aceitunas

Fish with Tomatoes, Capers and Olives

4 white fish fillets, 150g/5oz each (such as monkfish) • juice of 1 lime • salt • 125ml/4fl oz/½ cup corn oil • 2 onions, sliced • 2 cloves garlic, finely chopped • 10 ripe tomatoes, roasted, skinned and chopped • 1 pickled Jalapeño chilli, without stalk or seeds, cut into thin strips • 2 tbsp fresh mixed herbs, coarsely chopped • 2 tbsp fresh flat-leaf parsley, chopped • 20 pitted green olives, chopped • 2 tbsp large bottled capers, drained • 2 bay leaves • ¼ tsp black peppercorns, crushed • 250ml/8fl oz/1 cup light fish stock • sprigs of fresh parsley, to garnish

TIP For this recipe you can also cook the fish in the oven. Place the fillets in a greased oven-proof dish, spoon the sauce over it and cover with foil. Bake the fish in a preheated oven at 180°C/gas mark 4/350°F for 10 minutes or until cooked. You can also do this with whole fish, such as trout, mullet or gurnard. Score the fish beforehand and stew it for a little longer, or until cooked.

1. Rinse the fish fillets, pat them dry and place in a non-metallic dish. Sprinkle with lime juice and salt. Cover the dish and leave in the fridge for 1 hour.
2. Heat the oil in a frying pan, add the onion rings and fry until golden brown.
3. Stir the garlic through the onion rings, leave to fry for 1 minute, then add the tomatoes. Simmer gently for 5 minutes.
4. Add the Jalapeño chilli, herbs, 15 olives, 1 tablespoon capers, the bay leaves and black pepper.
5. Pour the stock into the mixture and bring to the boil. Lower the heat and leave to simmer gently for 10 minutes, then season with salt.
6. Take the fish out of the fridge and rinse with cold water. Put the fish into the tomato sauce and ensure it is fully covered. Increase the heat slightly and leave to cook quite gently for 10 minutes.
7. Serve the fish on warmed serving plates with the sauce spooned over. Garnish with the rest of the olives and capers and a few sprigs of parsley. Serve immediately with cooked rice.

Trucha con Pacán

Trout with Pecan Nuts

2 fresh Pasilla chillies or 2 fresh Jalapeño chillies • 4 cloves garlic, halved lengthways • 2 tbsp fresh oregano, chopped • juice of 2 limes • salt • 4 whole trout, cleaned • butter, for greasing • 50g/2oz flaked almonds • 50g/2oz pecan nuts, chopped

1 Roast the chillies in a dry frying pan, but make sure the outside of the chillies doesn't burn. Remove the chillies from the pan, put them in a plastic food bag and close tightly. Leave to rest for 20 minutes.
2 Take the chillies out of the bag and remove and discard the skin, stalk and seeds. Chop the flesh very finely.
3 Put the chillies in a shallow non-metallic dish that the trout fits into. Add the garlic, oregano, lime juice and some salt and mix well. Coat each trout in the spice mixture and place them in the dish. Cover and leave the fish to marinade for 30 minutes. Turn the trout after 15 minutes.
4 Preheat the oven to 200°C/gas mark 6/400°F. Cut 4 pieces of foil each big enough to wrap one trout. Butter the pieces of foil on the inside.
5 Place each trout on a piece of buttered foil, sprinkle with the marinade, then finally sprinkle with the almonds and pecan nuts. Close the foil over the trout to make 4 parcels.
6 Place on a baking tray and bake in the oven for 25 minutes or until cooked. Remove the foil and serve immediately.

86

TIP Roasting chillies is a trick to release all the chilli's aroma and flavour. In addition, it is much easier to peel it. Do not roast them for too long, however, since the taste will become bitter.

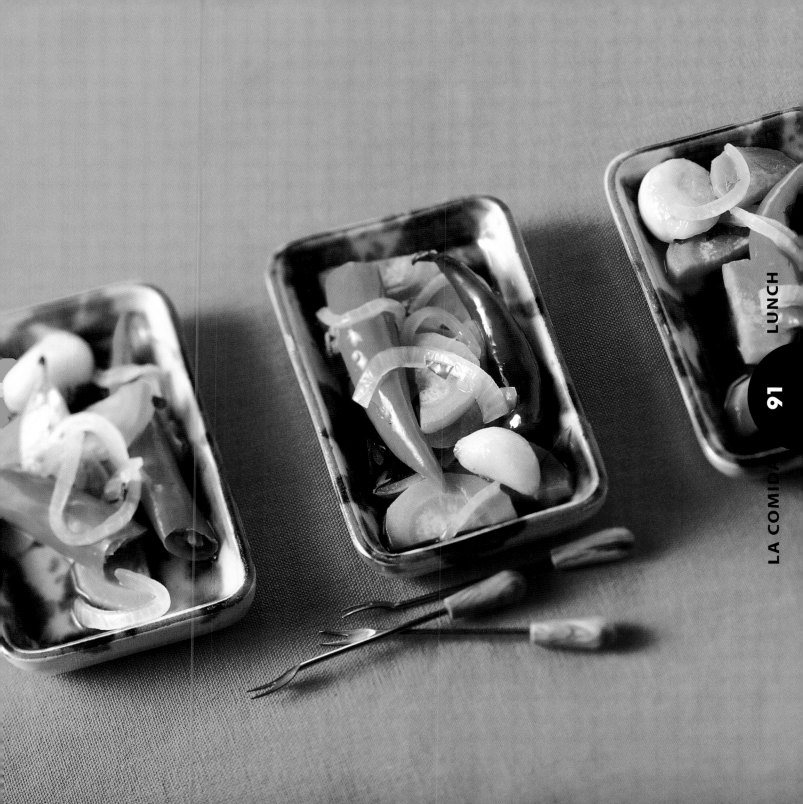

92

Burritos (receta básica)

Burritos (basic recipe)

350g/12oz plain flour • 75g/3oz soft vegetable margarine • 1 tsp salt • 150ml/5fl oz/¾ cup lukewarm water

1   Mix the flour and margarine together in a bowl using your fingertips, until the mixture resembles breadcrumbs. Add the salt and water and knead into a firm dough.
2   Leave the dough to rest for 30 minutes, so that it becomes easier to roll it out.
3   Divide the dough into 10-12 equal pieces and roll into balls. Roll the balls of dough on a floured surface to form flat rounds, each about 18cm/7in in diameter.
4   Fry the burritos, one at a time, without fat, in a hot, large, heavy-based frying pan for about ½ minute on each side. Do not allow the pan to get too hot. They're ready when they puff up. Keep the cooked burritos warm (see box) while you finish cooking the others.

TIP Store the burritos under a (damp) cloth, with non-stick baking paper in between, if you wish, before you fill them.

Burritos con Carne de Cerdo

Burritos with Pork

10–12 burritos: see basic recipe (p. 92) • 400g/14oz lean pork fillet, cubed • juice of 3 oranges • juice of 3 limes • 6 tbsp corn oil • 1 large onion, sliced • 2 cloves garlic, crushed • 1 fresh Poblano chilli or 2 fresh green Lombok chillies, deseeded and cut into rings • 150g/5oz plums, stones removed, chopped • salt and freshly ground black pepper

94

TIP The juice of the Seville or bitter orange is often used in Mexican dishes. This citrus fruit is difficult to find in some parts of Europe. This dish combines orange with lime, giving the flavour a bit more character. For those who love a more bitter flavour, adding some grapefruit juice works well.

1 Place the pork in a pan and pour over the orange and lime juices, ensuring the meat is covered. Bring to the boil, then lower the heat, cover and cook until the meat is tender (about 40 minutes).
2 Remove the meat from the pan to a plate, leave to cool slightly, then tear into shreds. If necessary, make it even finer by processing it in a blender or food processor or by grinding it with a pestle and mortar. Set aside. Discard the juices in the pan.
3 Heat the oil in a frying pan, add the onion and garlic and fry until softened. Add the chilli, plums and meat. Fry until the meat darkens, stirring regularly. Season with salt and pepper. Keep hot.
4 Meanwhile, heat the burritos (wrapped in foil) in a preheated oven at 170ºC/gas mark 3/325ºF for 15 minutes. Spoon a small pile of pork mixture onto each burrito and fold them in half. If necessary, secure with cocktail sticks. Serve hot with guacamole (see p. 30).

Burritos con Carne de Vaca Sazonadas y Salsa de Pimienta y Tomate

Burritos with Spiced Beef and Chilli Tomato Sauce

10-12 Burritos: see basic recipe (p. 92) • 400g/14oz brisket or stewing beef, cubed • 1 onion, halved • 2 cloves garlic • 1 fresh Poblano chilli, deseeded and chopped • 2 tsp cumin seeds • 2 tsp ground cinnamon • 1-1½ litres/1¾-2½ pints water • For the chilli tomato sauce: • 1 tsp corn oil • 1 onion, chopped • 2 fresh Serrano or Fresno chillies, deseeded and chopped • 5 tomatoes, skinned and chopped • salt and freshly ground black pepper

1   Put the beef, onion, garlic, chilli, cumin seeds, cinnamon and water in a pan and bring to the boil over a medium heat. Lower the heat, then cover and leave to simmer for 1 hour or until the meat is very soft, regularly skimming the scum off the top.
2   Take the pan off the heat and leave the meat to cool in the liquid. Remove the meat from the liquid and pull it to shreds with a fork. Keep 250ml/8fl oz/1 cup of the cooking liquid for the sauce. Set aside.
3   For the sauce, heat the oil in a frying pan over a high heat, add the onion and chillies and sauté for 3 minutes, stirring continuously, until soft.
4   Stir in the tomatoes and the reserved cooking liquid. Gently bring the mixture to the boil and leave to simmer for 10 minutes, until the sauce thickens. Season with salt and pepper.
5   Add the shredded meat to the sauce and leave to simmer until piping hot.
6   Meanwhile, wrap the burritos in foil, then heat them in a preheated oven at 170ºC/gas mark 3/325ºF for 15 minutes. Spoon some beef filling onto each burrito and fold them up. If necessary, secure with cocktail sticks. Serve immediately.

TIP Instead of Serrano chillies you can also use Madame Jeanette chillies. In that case, leave them whole and cook with the sauce. Take them out before serving (do not eat these chillies: they are awfully hot).

96

Burrito con Carne de Vaca y Huevo Revuelto

Burritos with Beef and Scrambled Eggs

10-12 burritos: see basic recipe (p. 92) • 200g/7oz stewing steak, cubed • 2 onions, chopped • salt • 6 tbsp corn oil • 4 fresh Serrano chillies or 2 fresh Lombok chillies, deseeded and finely chopped • 1 large tomato, roasted, skinned and chopped • 6 large eggs, beaten

1 Place the meat in a pan and add enough water until the meat is covered. Add one of the onions and some salt and bring to the boil, then cover and simmer until the meat is tender (about 40 minutes). Remove the pan from the heat.
2 Leave the meat to cool in the liquid, then remove and cut into small pieces. Next, shred the pieces. If necessary, grind the meat with a pestle or mortar or process it in a blender or food processor to soften it. Set aside.
3 Heat the oil in a frying pan, add the remaining onion, the chillies and tomato and fry over a medium heat for about 5 minutes.
4 Add the meat and fry for about 5 minutes, stirring continuously, until brown.
5 Add the eggs and cook until they are just cooked and scrambled, stirring continuously (do not overcook because the eggs will become too dry). Keep hot.
6 Meanwhile, wrap the burritos in foil and heat them in a preheated oven at 170ºC/gas mark 3/325ºF for 15 minutes. Spoon some beef filling onto each burrito and fold them up. If necessary, secure with cocktail sticks. Serve immediately.

WAR The fact that the war between the US and Mexico did not have the happiest of endings for the latter is quite clear from the amount of land that Mexico has had to surrender. American states such as Texas and Arizona used to belong to Mexico.

Burrito con Queso Feta y Arroz

Burritos with Feta and Rice

10-12 Burritos: see basic recipe (p. 92) • 1 dried chilli (such as Chipotle chillies), deseeded • 90g/3½oz white rice with a small, round grain (such as Arborio) • 3 tbsp corn oil • 1 small onion, chopped • 75g/3oz flaked almonds • 2 tomatoes, skinned and chopped • 1 tbsp fresh oregano, chopped • 1 tsp fresh thyme, chopped • 200g/7oz feta cheese, crumbled • 1-2 spring onions, sliced (for garnishing) • 1 lime, cut into segments (for garnishing)

100

TIP Because lunch is the most important and biggest meal of the day, the restaurants offer a set menu with various courses in the afternoon. This *Comida* is usually reasonably priced and the ideal way to get to know the Mexican cuisine. The Mexicans themselves take plenty of time to enjoy lunch, which often stretches to 2-3 hours. We should learn from their example!

1 Pour hot water over the dried chilli in a bowl and leave to soak for 1 hour. Drain, then purée the chilli in a blender or food processor.
2 Meanwhile, boil the rice in a pan of boiling water until slightly undercooked (about 15 minutes). Drain well and set aside.
3 Heat the oil in a pan, add the onion and sauté until soft and translucent. Add the chilli paste and fry for 5 minutes.
4 Add the rice and almonds and stir the mixture thoroughly. Add the tomatoes and their juice. Bring the mixture to the boil and simmer until the juice has evaporated and the rice is cooked. Stir in the oregano, thyme and feta, then take the pan off the heat.
5 Meanwhile, wrap the burritos in foil, and heat them in a preheated oven at 170ºC/gas mark 3/325ºF for 15 minutes. Spoon some feta filling onto each burrito and fold them up. If necessary, secure with cocktail sticks. Garnish with the spring onions and lime segments. Serve immediately with a green salad.

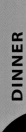

DINNER

103

LA CENA

La Cena

Licor de Fresas

Strawberry Liqueur

500g/1¼lb strawberries, halved (plus extra for garnishing) • 250ml/8fl oz/1 cup tequila • zest of 1 lemon, cut into narrow strips • ½ bunch fresh mint, coarsely chopped

PURE Tequila is made from the juice of a special blue agave, a plant with long, spiky leaves. People often think this is a cactus, which is based on a misunderstanding: the agave and the cactus are both crassula plants, but of totally different families. Tequila is a strong drink with about 40% alcohol, but it seems to be one of the healthiest distilled drinks, because it is so pure. Cheers!

1   Put the strawberries in a large clean, sterilised jar with a lid that seals well. Pour the tequila over the strawberries until they are fully covered. Add the lemon zest.
2   Close the jar and leave to stand in a cool dry place for at least 2 weeks.
3   Strain the contents of the jar through a sieve, reserving the liquid. Drink the strained liqueur cold, in glasses, garnished with mint and fresh strawberries.

Ensalada de Gambas

Prawn Salad

400g/14oz cooked, peeled prawns • juice of 1 lime • salt and freshly ground black pepper • 3 tomatoes, skinned and cut into 1½cm/¾in pieces • 1 ripe, firm avocado, peeled, stoned and cut into 1cm/½in cubes • 2 handfuls lamb's lettuce • 150ml/5fl oz/¾ cup soured cream • strips of green pepper, to garnish • For the dressing: 1 tbsp lime juice • 150ml/5fl oz/¾ cup corn oil • 1 tbsp fresh coriander, coarsely chopped

WATER Mexico is wedged between the Pacific Ocean and the Gulf of Mexico, which is connected to the Atlantic Ocean. More than 9000 kilometres of coast altogether! It is therefore no surprise that crustaceans and shellfish are often on the menu.

1 Place the prawns in a large, non-metallic dish and add the lime juice, salt and pepper. Toss lightly to mix, then leave to marinade in a cool place for 2 hours.
2 Add the tomatoes and avocado to the prawns. Stir gently to mix.
3 Make the dressing by whisking together all the dressing ingredients in a small bowl.
4 Arrange the lettuce leaves on a serving dish and place the prawn mixture on top. Spoon the soured cream and dressing over the top. Garnish with strips of pepper. Serve.

This salad is delicious served with fresh crusty bread.

Ensalada de Verduras con Aliño de Ajo

Vegetables with a Garlic Dressing

500g/1¼lb fresh spinach, washed • 300g/11oz green beans • 3 courgettes, cut into large, thick strips • 100g/4oz shelled peas, fresh or frozen • salt • 1 red onion, sliced • For the garlic dressing: 6 cloves garlic, unpeeled • 120ml/4fl oz/½ cup corn oil • 6 tbsp white wine vinegar • freshly ground black pepper • 2 tbsp fresh flat-leaf parsley, chopped • caster sugar to taste

1   Briefly blanch the spinach in its own water in a large pan. Drain well, squeezing out excess liquid. Blanch the beans, courgettes and peas separately in a large pan of boiling water with a pinch of salt, until they start to change colour. Drain the vegetables and place them on a serving dish.
2   For the dressing, dry-fry the garlic in a pan over a high heat until the skin has blackened. Leave to cool slightly, then peel the cloves.
3   Purée the garlic, oil, vinegar and black pepper to taste in a blender or food processor. Stir in the parsley and season to taste with salt and sugar.
4   Spoon the dressing over the vegetables and garnish with the red onion rings. Serve immediately.

TIP Raw onion *(cebolla)* is the most popular flavouring for many Mexican dishes. In each kitchen you will find dishes of chopped onion for putting on salads and other vegetable dishes. Mexicans especially love to put red onion in their food.

Lentejas con Carne de Cerdo

Lentils with Pork

250g/9oz lean pork, cubed • 250g/9oz green lentils • 150g/5oz raisins • 2 tbsp corn oil • 1 onion, finely chopped • 2 cloves garlic, chopped • 1 apple, peeled, cored and chopped • 2 rings of canned pine-apple, chopped • 5 tomatoes, skinned, deseeded and chopped • 1 banana, peeled and chopped • 1 fresh Jalapeño chilli, deseeded and chopped • salt

1   Place the pork in a pan, cover with water and bring to the boil. Lower the heat, cover and simmer for 30-45 minutes.
2   Drain the meat (save the liquid), cover and set aside.
3   Clean the pan and pour the cooking liquid back into the pan. Add the lentils and raisins. Add extra water if the lentils aren't fully submerged. Bring to the boil, then lower the heat and simmer gently for about 30-45 minutes, until the lentils are cooked. If necessary, add a little more (boiling) water. Drain the lentils and raisins. Set aside.
4   Meanwhile, heat the oil in a frying pan, add the cooked pork, onion and garlic and fry until the meat is slightly browned. Remove everything from the pan with a slotted spoon, and add to the lentils and raisins. Set aside and keep warm.
5   Fry the apple and pineapple in the remaining oil in the frying pan for a few minutes. Add the tomatoes, banana and chilli and season with salt. Boil the mixture until all the liquid has disappeared, stirring regularly.
6   Fold the fruit mixture carefully through the lentil mixture. Return the mixture to the pan and cook for about 5 minutes over a low heat, uncovered, until you have a fairly dry consistency, with creamy lentils. Serve immediately.

This is also delicious mixed with finely diced chorizo, before serving.

PEPPER SAUSAGE The chorizo mentioned at the end of the recipe is Spanish chorizo, with a flavour that goes really well with this dish. Mexican chorizo is a strongly spiced, fresh pork sausage that has to be cooked first. If you manage to get hold of it, take care, because the chillies in the sausage can be pretty hot!

Ensalada de Calabacín

Courgette Salad

6 young courgettes, thickly sliced • salt and freshly ground black pepper • 100ml/4fl oz/½ cup corn oil • 3 tbsp white wine vinegar • 1 bunch spring onions • 2 avocados, peeled, stoned and diced • 1 fresh Poblano chilli or fresh green Lombok chilli, deseeded and cut into strips

PROTECTION Chillies are hot because of capsaicin, most of which is located in the membranes and the seeds. This is why we usually remove these. When cutting away the membranes, use disposable gloves or, if you don't have any, simply use a sandwich bag 'worn' over each hand. This way you will prevent yourself from later rubbing your eyes with fingers covered in hot chilli juice. A painful experience you definitely want to avoid!

1 Boil the courgette slices in a pan of plenty of boiling water, with a pinch of salt, for 6-8 minutes. The courgettes should be *al dente*. Drain, pat the slices dry, then cut them into large pieces and leave them to cool.
2 Make a vinaigrette by whisking together the oil and vinegar in a small bowl. Season with salt and pepper.
3 Place all the ingredients, except for the chilli, in a serving bowl and mix with the vinaigrette. Leave to cool in the fridge.
4 Garnish with strips of chilli, just before serving.

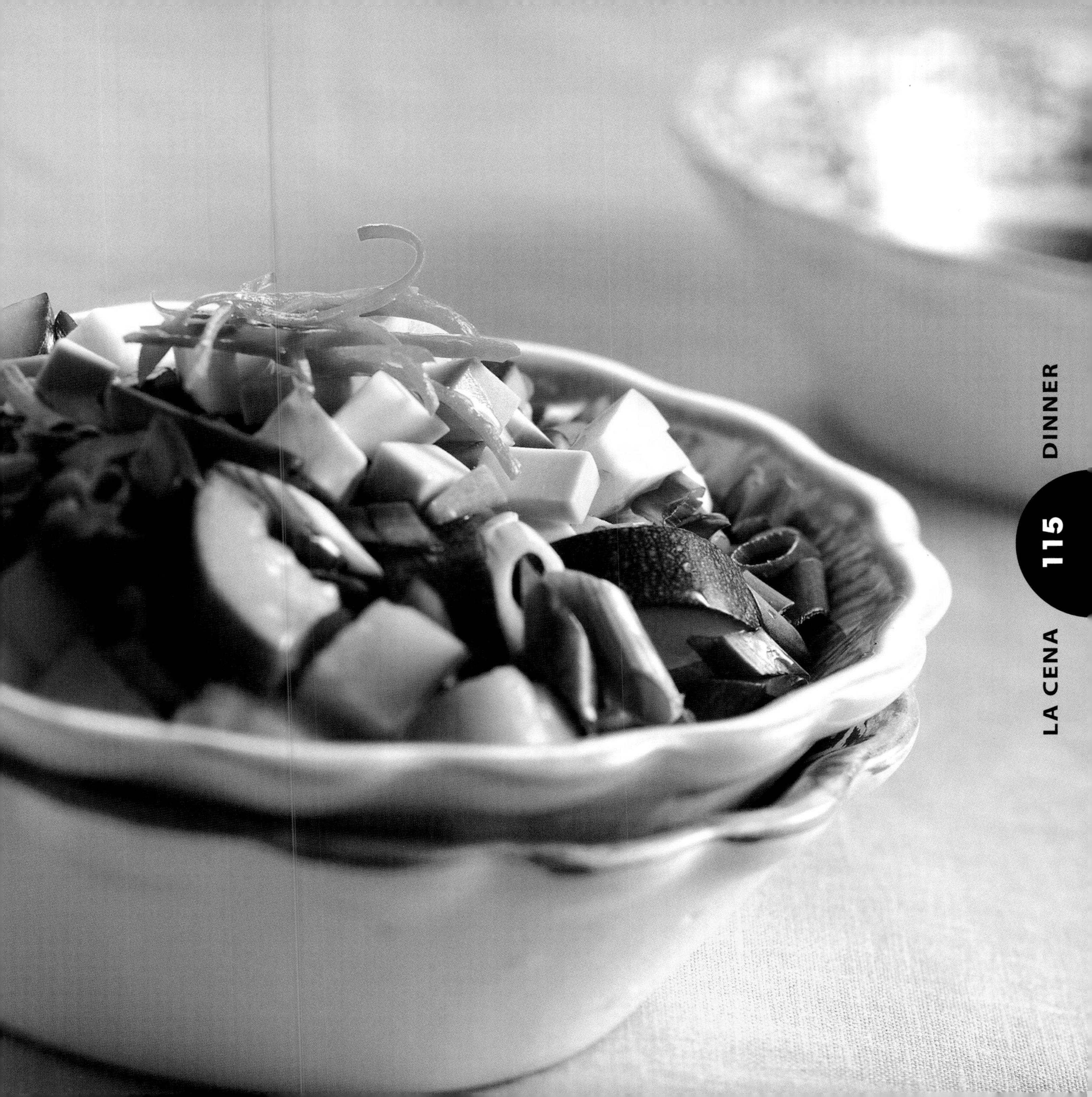

Calabacín con Ajo

Courgettes with Garlic

6 young courgettes, diced • 1 tsp salt • 2 tbsp corn oil • 5 cloves garlic, sliced • ¼ tsp freshly ground black pepper • 2 tbsp fresh flat-leaf parsley, coarsely chopped • juice of ½ lime • salt, to taste • 1 tbsp fresh oregano, coarsely chopped

1 Put the courgettes into a colander, sprinkle with 1 teaspoon salt and shake briefly. Leave the courgettes aside for 10 minutes.
2 Rinse the courgettes with cold water and pat dry with kitchen paper. Set aside.
3 Heat the oil in a frying pan, add the garlic and fry until lightly browned.
4 Remove the garlic from the pan using a slotted spoon and set aside to drain. Briefly stir-fry the courgettes in the remaining oil in the pan until the cubes are lightly browned but still crunchy.
5 Mix together the garlic, courgettes, pepper and parsley in a serving bowl. Sprinkle with lime juice and season with salt, if necessary. Mix everything together well and garnish with the oregano. Serve.

Plátanos Sazonados Fritos

Spiced Fried Plantains

juice of 2 limes • 2 large plantains, peeled and sliced • 30g/ 1oz butter • ½ tsp chilli powder • 2 tbsp caster sugar • 1 tsp ground cinnamon

1 Pour the juice of the limes over the slices of plantain in a dish.
2 Heat the butter in a small pan until melted, then fry the plantain slices in small batches, ensuring the temperature in the pan does not lower too much.
3 Once the plantain slices are golden brown, remove them from the pan with a slotted spoon and drain on kitchen paper. Keep warm. Repeat until all the plantain slices are cooked.
4 Mix together the chilli powder, sugar and cinnamon in a small bowl. Place the warm plantain slices on a serving plate, sprinkle with the chilli-cinnamon mix and serve immediately.

Seviche con Limón

Marinaded Fish with Lime

500g/1¼lb fresh, firm tuna steaks, cut into strips • juice of 8 limes • 3 ripe tomatoes, oven-roasted and chopped • 4 pickled Jalapeño chillies or 1 fresh green Lombok chilli, chopped • 4 cloves garlic, crushed • 100ml/4fl oz/½ cup corn oil • ½ onion, finely diced • 3 tbsp pitted green olives, chopped • 2 tbsp fresh coriander leaves, chopped

MARINADE It may sound rather odd, but putting fish in a marinade actually cooks it. You will see that the translucent flesh becomes opaque, as if it has been cooked. It is therefore interesting to know that the word "marinade" comes from the word "marine": the salty sea water was once used to marinade products, so they would keep longer.

1   Place the tuna in a bowl, pour over the lime juice and leave to marinade for 3 hours in the fridge, until the fish is opaque. Stir occasionally.
2   Pour off half the lime juice, then add the tomatoes, chillies, garlic and oil to the fish. Stir thoroughly and chill for a further 1 hour. Remove from the refrigerator 20 minutes before serving, to allow it to come up to room temperature.
3   Before serving, sprinkle over the onion, olives and coriander.

You can also make this dish with firm white fish, such as hake or Pollack.

Tortillas de Maíz (receta básica)

Corn Tortillas (basic recipe)

250g/9oz masa harina: see recipe (p. 8) • 1 tsp salt • 275ml/½ pint/ 1 cup lukewarm water

1   Mix the masa harina maize flour and salt together in a bowl, then mix in the water, stirring continuously. Knead to create a firm dough that no longer sticks to the hands. Leave to rest for 30 minutes.
2   Shape the dough into 12 ping-pong-ball-sized balls.
3   Roll them out on non-stick baking paper to make flat rounds of dough about 15cm/5in in diameter.
4   Fry the tortillas, one at a time, in a dry frying pan, for 20-30 seconds on each side. Store the cooked tortillas under a (damp) cloth, with non-stick baking paper inbetween each one, if you wish, before you fill them.

Enchiladas Rellenas de Pollo con Salsa de Tomatillo

Chicken-filled Enchiladas with Tomatillo Sauce

12 corn tortillas: see basic recipe (p. 122) • Salsa Verde: see recipe (p. 32) and prepare three times as much for the enchiladas • 2 large, skinless boneless chicken breasts, poached and torn into pieces • 4 tbsp crème fraîche • 1 tbsp finely chopped onion • salt • 40g/1½oz Mexican queso anejo (or a slightly matured Gouda, Gruyere or feta cheese), crumbled or diced • 1 red onion, sliced

1 Heat the salsa verde in a pan over a low heat. Preheat the oven to 180ºC/gas mark 4/350ºF.
2 In another pan, heat the chicken in a little water, until hot.
3 Mix the chicken with the crème fraîche, chopped onion and a good pinch of salt. Cool, then cover the dish and chill in the fridge until ready to use.
4 Heat the tortillas in a steamer set over a pan of boiling water and keep them warm.
5 Pour about 400ml/14fl oz/1¾ cup hot salsa verde onto a large, deep plate. Place a tortilla in the sauce, turn it over, then spoon over 2 tablespoons of the chicken mixture in a line down the middle and roll the tortilla up. Place it in an oven proof dish, then do the same with all the other tortillas. Pour the rest of the salsa verde over the enchiladas (make sure that the ends of the rolls are covered with the sauce).
6 Immediately cover the dish with foil and put it in the oven for 5-10 minutes or until the contents are piping hot. Sprinkle the enchiladas with the cheese and garnish with red onion rings. Serve immediately.

124

FRESH AND CREAMY

Crema Espesa is the Mexican name for crème fraîche. If you do not have any crème fraîche, it is also nice to take a thick cream and sour it with buttermilk or a little lemon juice. The fresh taste is one of the typical Mexican flavours.

Enchiladas con Queso, Verduras y Salsa de Guindilla Roja

Enchiladas with Cheese, Vegetables and Red Chilli Sauce

12 corn tortillas: see basic recipe (p. 122) • 30g/1oz dried Guajillo chillies, stalks, seeds and membranes removed • 100g/4oz dried Ancho chillies or 2 fresh green Lombok chillies, deseeded • 4 large cloves garlic, unpeeled • ¼ tsp black peppercorns, crushed • ⅓ tsp ground cumin • 2 large waxy potatoes, peeled and cut into 1cm/½in cubes • 250g/9oz carrots, cut into 1cm/½in pieces • 3 tbsp white wine vinegar • 1 tsp salt • oil, for frying • ½ onion, sliced • 50g/2oz crumbled Mexican queso fresco (or feta or goat's cheese)

1   Tear the dried chillies into flat pieces and grill in a pan or on a baking tray under a preheated grill until they start changing colour and become crisp. Add the garlic cloves and grill until their skins are blackened.
2   Put the grilled chillies in a bowl, pour over some boiling water, cover and leave to soak for 1 hour.
3   Peel the garlic cloves and put the flesh in a blender or food processor. Add the grilled chillies plus soaking water, peppercorns and cumin and blend until the mixture forms a sauce. Set aside.
4   For the vegetable filling, put the potatoes and carrots in a pan with water and add the vinegar and salt. Bring to the boil and cook for about 15 minutes, until tender, then drain and set aside.
5   Heat 3 tablespoons oil in a large frying pan or wok over a medium heat. Dip both sides of a tortilla in the chilli sauce. Fold the tortilla twice, so it looks like a quarter of a tortilla. Place it in the hot oil, turn the tortilla after 20 seconds, and fry the other side for 20 seconds too. Remove from the oil and keep hot in a preheated oven. Dip, fold and fry the rest of the tortillas in the same way.
6   Pour a small dash of oil into the frying pan or wok, add the potatoes, carrots and 2 or 3 tablespoons chilli sauce and stir-fry the vegetables for 3-4 minutes, until piping hot.
7   Place the hot enchiladas on a serving plate, spoon over the potato and carrot mixture and sprinkle with onion and cheese. Serve immediately.

Enchiladas con Espinacas y Queso

Enchiladas with Spinach and Cheese

12 corn tortillas: see basic recipe (p. 122) • For the sauce: 1 tbsp corn oil • 2 cloves garlic, chopped • 2 tomatoes, skinned and chopped • 1-2 fresh Poblano chillies or 4 fresh green Lombok chillies, deseeded and chopped • ½ tsp ground cumin • 1 tbsp fresh oregano, chopped • salt and pepper • For the filling: 2 tsp corn oil • 1 onion, chopped • 2 fresh green or red Lombok chillies, deseeded and chopped • 1 tsp cumin seeds • 250g/9oz fresh spinach • 3 tomatoes, skinned and chopped • 150g/5oz feta cheese, crumbled • 170g/6oz strong cheese, grated (such as fresh Parmesan)

1   For the sauce, heat the oil in a pan, add the garlic and sauté gently for a few minutes. Add the tomatoes, chillies, cumin and oregano. Cook until reduced to a fairly thick sauce, then season with salt and pepper. Keep warm.
2   For the filling, heat the oil in a non-stick frying pan over a medium heat. Add the onion, chillies and cumin seeds and sauté, stirring continuously, until the onion is golden and softened. Add the spinach and tomatoes and cook for 4 minutes until the spinach wilts and the mixture is piping hot, stirring regularly.
3   Stir in the feta and 150g/5oz of the strong cheese. Keep warm. Preheat the oven to 180°C/gas mark 4/350°F.
4   Fry the tortillas, one at a time, in a dry frying pan over a medium heat for 20-30 seconds on each side, until they are hot. Remove from the pan, spoon on some spinach filling and some tomato sauce, and roll up the tortillas. Put the enchiladas in an oven proof dish, then do the same with the rest of the tortillas, reserving a little of the tomato sauce.
5   Pour the reserved tomato sauce over the enchiladas. Sprinkle with the remaining strong cheese, then put the dish in the oven and bake for 5-10 minutes until hot. Serve immediately.

128

CONFUSING! The Mexican word "salsa" looks a bit like our word "sauce". However, salsa is usually a chunky or mashed mixture of various ingredients. These salsas can contain tomatoes, tomatillos, chillies, onion, garlic, etc, and are really something that hovers between a chunky sauce and a salad.

Enchiladas de Carne de Vaca con Salsa Roja y Salsa de Mango

Beef Enchiladas with Red Sauce and Mango Salsa

8 corn tortillas: see basic recipe (p. 122), reduce quantity by half • 500g/1¼lb lean beef, cut into 5cm/2in cubes • 2 dried red Lombok chillies, deseeded • 2 tbsp corn oil • 2 cloves garlic, crushed • 1 small onion, finely chopped • 2 tsp fresh oregano, coarsely chopped • ½ tsp ground cumin • 1 tsp lime juice • 50g/2oz strong cheese, grated (such as fresh Parmesan) • For the mango salsa: 1 red onion, coarsely chopped • 1 large ripe mango, peeled, stoned and coarsely chopped • juice of 1 lime • salt and freshly ground black pepper

1 Place the beef in a pan and cover with water. Bring to the boil, then turn down the heat and leave to simmer for 1–1½ hours, until the meat is very tender.
2 Meanwhile, pour boiling water over the dried chillies in a bowl and leave to soak for 30 minutes. Put the chillies and their soaking liquid in a blender or food processor and blend to a smooth paste. Set aside.
3 Drain the meat and let it cool. Save 250ml/8fl oz/1 cup of the cooking liquid.
4 Heat the oil in a pan, add the garlic, onion, oregano and cumin and fry for about 2 minutes.
5 Stir the lime juice, chilli paste and the reserved cooking liquid through the garlic mixture. Simmer gently for about 10 minutes, stirring occasionally, until the sauce has thickened.
6 Shred the beef with 2 forks, stir it through the chilli sauce and cook for another few minutes.
7 For the salsa, mix together the onion, mango and lime juice and season with salt and pepper. Set aside.
8 Fry the tortillas, one at a time, in a hot, dry frying pan, for 20-30 seconds on each side. Spoon some meat mixture onto each tortilla and roll into an enchilada. Keep the filled enchiladas hot in a preheated oven until they are all made.
9 Garnish the enchiladas with the cheese and serve with the mango salsa.

Enchiladas con Carne de Cerdo y Mole

Enchiladas with Pork and Mole

8-10 corn tortillas: **see basic recipe (p. 122), reduce quantity by one third • 500g/1¼lb pork loin, cut into 1½cm/¾in cubes • 1 dried Chipotle chilli • 2 tbsp corn oil • 2 cloves garlic, crushed • 1 clove garlic, coarsely chopped • 1 onion, finely chopped • 5 tomatoes, skinned and chopped • 4 tbsp sesame seeds, toasted • 1 tsp paprika • 1 tsp ground cumin • 25g/1oz unsweetened cocoa powder • 1 ripe avocado, peeled, stoned and diced**

1 Put the pork in a pan, cover with water and bring to the boil. Lower the heat and leave to simmer for about 40 minutes.
2 Meanwhile, soak the dried chilli in hot water in a small bowl for 30 minutes. Drain, then remove the membranes and stalks. Set aside.
3 Drain the pork and leave it to cool, then shred it using 2 forks. Set aside.
4 Heat the oil in a frying pan, then add the garlic and onion and fry for 3-4 minutes, until the onion is translucent. Chop the chilli and add it to the onion and garlic, together with the shredded pork. Heat gently until hot, stirring regularly.
5 Meanwhile, preheat the oven to 180ºC/gas mark 4/350ºF. Soften the tortillas by wrapping them in foil and steaming them on a plate over a pan of boiling water.
6 Spoon 2 tablespoons of the pork mixture onto the middle of each tortilla and roll each one up to form an enchilada. Place the enchiladas in a shallow, oven proof dish, large enough to put all the enchiladas next to each other in one single layer. Keep hot.
7 Purée the tomatoes, sesame seeds, paprika and cumin together in a blender or food processor. Heat this purée gently in a pan, then add the cocoa powder and cook until it has thickened, stirring regularly.
8 Pour the tomato sauce over the enchiladas until they are completely covered. Put the dish in the oven for 10-15 minutes, until piping hot. Serve garnished with the diced avocado.

132

COLOURFUL The aboriginal Mexican Indian natives are true artists where the weaving of cloth is concerned. Each area has its own colours and patterns. Connoisseurs know exactly in which village a certain fabric was produced.

135

Fiesta

Margarita

Margarita

1 lime segment • coarse salt • 6 tbsp tequila • 2 tbsp Cointreau • 2 tbsp triple sec • 2-4 tbsp lime juice • 7 ice cubes

138

WORLD FAMOUS The world famous Margarita cocktail was first mixed by Pancho Morales in 1942. You can't get any more Mexican than that. According to the story, a woman came into his bar in Chihuahua and ordered an unknown cocktail. Of course he offered her an alternative, which he made up on the spot. The mix of tequila, Cointreau and lime juice was so excellent, that the woman in question wished to know its name. This was made up on the spot too, and the Margarita started its victory march all around the world.

1 Rub the rim of 2 cocktail glasses with the rind of the lime and dip them in salt, creating a layer of salt on the rim of each glass.
2 Mix the tequila with the, Cointreau, triple sec, lime juice and ice cubes in a cocktail shaker until the ice cubes have melted.
3 Pour into 2 cocktail glasses and serve.

Tequila Sunrise

Tequila Sunrise

slug of grenadine in a bowl • caster sugar on a saucer • 1½ tbsp grenadine syrup • 100ml/4fl oz/½ cup tequila, chilled • 1½ tbsp lime juice • fresh orange juice, chilled • 2 slices of orange

HAMMOCK Mexico is hammock country. And not just in the funny cliché of a Mexican with a sombrero holding a siesta, but in real life too! The hammock was invented here, and there isn't a country in the world that has as many hammocks as Mexico. How about finding out why, try mixing a Tequila Sunrise, and lazing about in a hammock for a bit!

1   If you wish, dip the rim of the cocktail glasses in some grenadine and then in the sugar, creating a pink rim.
2   Pour the grenadine syrup into the glasses.
3   Carefully pour in the tequila and lime juice (pour it over the back of a spoon into each glass).
4   Slowly finish with orange juice. Try to keep the drink layers separate. This way, the cocktails will look like a sunrise.
5   Garnish each cocktail with a slice of orange and serve immediately.

Rompope

Rompope (Rum Drink)

1 litre full fat milk • 1 vanilla pod, split in half lengthways • 12 large egg yolks • 180g/6oz caster sugar • 250ml/8fl oz/1 cup white rum • freshly grated nutmeg

TIP Rum is a spirit that became known mainly through the Caribbean. It is not made of blue agave, such as with tequila, but of sugar cane, and there is plenty of sugar cane available in Mexico. Therefore, a huge amount of rum is produced each year. Incidentally, in these parts, the drink, which is ideal for mixers, is called *ron*.

1 Put the milk and vanilla pod in a large pan and bring gently to the boil. Leave the mixture to simmer gently over a low heat for 15 minutes, stirring continuously.
2 Turn off the heat and remove the vanilla pod.
3 Whisk the egg yolks with the sugar in a bowl until they are lightly coloured, then stir into the milk mixture. Bring gently to the boil once again, stirring continuously, until the mixture starts to thicken and coats the spoon. Remove from the heat and leave to cool.
4 Once cool, stir in the rum.
5 Pour the mixture into a large, clean, sterilised bottle or jar, close it tightly and refrigerate for 8 hours.
6 Serve chilled in glasses and garnish with grated nutmeg, just before serving.

Banana Daiquiri

Banana Daiquiri

200ml/7fl oz/¾ cup white rum • 3 tbsp crème de banane • juice of 2 limes • 2 bananas, peeled and mashed • 24 ice cubes

PARTY Why not organise a party with a Mexican finger food buffet and accompanying mixer drinks. Remember to have sufficient ice, a variety of glasses, a shaker, and especially lots of fruit. Fruit is not only essential for garnishing, but is also squeezed or puréed for mixers. A definite must are coconut and pineapple juice. After all, these are combined with rum to make the beach cocktail Piña Colada.

1 Mix together all the ingredients. Shake them in a cocktail shaker until the ice cubes have melted.
2 Strain the liqueur into cocktail glasses and serve with a straw.

Guindillas Rellenas de Salsa de Nueces

Stuffed Chillies with Walnut Sauce

6 large fresh Poblano chillies or sweet green chillies (or large Turkish or Moroccan chillies) • For the picadillo: 2 tbsp corn oil • 600g/1¼lb lean pork, finely chopped • ½ onion, chopped • 3 cloves garlic, chopped • 5 tomatoes, skinned and chopped • salt • 1 pear, peeled, cored and chopped • 2 tbsp raisins • 2 tbsp flaked almonds • For the sauce: 100g/4oz walnuts, soaked in milk for 8 hours, drained, patted dry and finely ground • 150g/5oz cream cheese, such as ricotta • 250g/9oz soured cream • ¼ tsp ground cinnamon (to taste) • For the batter: 2 large eggs, separated • ¼ tsp salt • plain flour, for dusting • oil, for deep-frying

1 Stick the chillies on a fork and hold them over a gas flame. Slowly turn until the skin starts blackening. Place the chillies in a plastic bag, seal the bag and leave to cool, then leave to rest for another 20 minutes.
2 Remove the skin from the chillies under cold running water. Carefully cut them lengthways on one side and remove the stalks, membranes and seeds. Leave the chillies as whole as possible. Set aside.
3 For the picadillo, heat the oil in a large frying pan, add the pork, and fry until it is slightly browned. Add the onion and garlic.
4 Once the onion has softened, add the tomatoes and season with salt. Simmer over a low heat for about 15 minutes.
5 Finally, add the pear, raisins and almonds and cook for another 5 minutes over a low heat. Remove the pan from the heat and leave the sauce to stand until you are ready to start stuffing the chillies.
6 For the sauce, mix the walnuts, cream cheese and soured cream together in a bowl until smooth. Add cinnamon to taste. Set aside.
7 For the batter, whisk the egg yolks in a bowl until they are light in colour. In another, grease-free bowl, whisk the egg whites with the salt until the mixture forms soft peaks. Gently fold the egg whites through the egg yolks.
8 Stuff the chillies with the picadillo, dust them with flour, then dip them in the egg mixture, covering them completely. Make sure that the pan with the oil for deep-frying is hot. Deep-fry the stuffed Poblanos until they are golden brown.
9 Remove the chillies from the hot oil using a slotted spoon, drain on kitchen paper, then put them on a serving dish and serve the walnut sauce separately.

These stuffed chillies are delicious when served with cooked rice or a salad.

Guindillas Rellenas de Salsa de Tomate

Stuffed Chillies with Tomato Sauce

6 large, fresh Poblano chillies or sweet green chillies (or large Turkish or Moroccan chillies) • 2 large eggs, separated • plain flour, for dusting • For the picadillo: corn oil, for frying • 4 cloves garlic, chopped • 600g/1¼lb lean beef, coarsely ground • 4 tomatoes, skinned and chopped • ½ tsp freshly ground black pepper • 2 tbsp flaked almonds • 1 tsp ground cinnamon • 5 cloves • salt • Tomato Sauce: see recipe (p. 34) • 250ml/8fl oz/1 cup chicken stock

MASHING AND CRUSHING The pestle and mortar *(moljacete)* is really an essential piece of kitchen equipment. The Mexicans use it to mash the basic ingredients for their sauces, such as chilli, garlic and tomatoes. A good pestle and mortar is made of stone and is heavy, so you are able to exert quite a bit of force. Of course, a blender or food processor will do, especially when dealing with larger quantities. The effect, however, is not quite the same, because a food processor throws the ingredients around and chops the food, and doesn't grind and mix it nice and slowly.

1 For the picadillo, heat a little oil in a pan, add the garlic and sauté until softened. Add the meat and fry until cooked, stirring regularly.
2 Add the tomatoes, pepper, almonds, cinnamon and cloves. Simmer gently until the liquid has evaporated and the sauce has reduced to a thick paste. Season with salt.
3 Meanwhile, roast the Poblanos over a gas flame until the skin blackens. Put them in a plastic food bag and leave to rest for 20 minutes. Remove the skin from the chillies under cold running water. Carefully cut the chillies lengthways on one side and remove the stalks, membranes and seeds. Leave the chillies as whole as possible. Put them aside until you are ready to stuff them.
4 Whisk the egg yolks in a bowl until they are lightly coloured. In another, grease-free bowl, whisk the egg whites with a good pinch of salt until the mixture forms soft peaks. Gently fold the egg whites through the egg yolks.
5 Stuff the chillies with the picadillo, dust them with flour, then dip them in the egg mixture, covering them completely.
6 Make sure that the pan with the oil for deep-frying is hot. Deep-fry the stuffed Poblanos until they are golden brown. Remove the chillies from the hot oil using a slotted spoon and drain on kitchen paper.
7 Meanwhile, heat the tomato sauce in a pan with the stock until the sauce has a consistency between a sauce and a soup. Carefully add the chillies. The chillies won't be completely covered by the sauce. Leave to cook over a low heat for a few more minutes, then serve hot.

Aguacete Relleno

Stuffed Avocado

4 large, ripe avocados • juice of 1 lime • 1 can (120g/4oz) sardines in olive oil • salt • freshly ground black pepper • 1 tbsp fresh coriander, finely chopped • about 2 tbsp white wine vinegar • 3 hard-boiled eggs, shelled, halved and chopped • 200g/7oz feta cheese, crumbled • 1 fresh Lombok chilli, sliced into rings

150

RIPE It is best to buy avocados a few days in advance. If they are still unripe and hard in the shop, they can ripen at home, for instance in a paper bag in a dark place. After 3-4 days they will be ripe and soft. If the avocados already have dark spots and feel soft in the shop, they are usually too far gone.

1 Peel and halve the avocados and remove the stones. Sprinkle with lime juice and set aside.
2 Mash the sardines together with the oil from the can in a bowl. Season with salt, pepper, coriander and a little vinegar. Add the eggs and mix well.
3 Spoon the sardine mixture into the hollows of the avocado halves, dividing it evenly.
4 Sprinkle with the feta cheese and chilli rings. Serve immediately.

Tomates Rellenos de Guacamole

Guacamole-Stuffed Tomatoes

6 large tomatoes, skinned • salt • 2 large avocados, peeled and stoned • ½ onion, chopped • 2 fresh Serrano chillies, deseeded and chopped • 1 tbsp fresh coriander, coarsely chopped • juice of ½ lime • extra coriander leaves, for garnishing

152

CALLING CARD Tomatoes as well as avocados originate from Mexico. The filling for this dish, the guacamole, has existed in several variations for the same amount of time as the avocado. Therefore, this wonderful little dish is basically the calling card of the Mexican cuisine.

1 Cut the tops off the tomatoes and carefully scoop out the flesh. Leave the sides fairly thick. Sprinkle the insides with salt and leave the tomatoes to drain upside down for 15 minutes.
2 Cut the tomato tops into small pieces for garnishing.
3 Mash the flesh of the avocados in a bowl and mix with the onion, chillies, chopped coriander and lime juice. Add salt to taste.
4 Spoon the guacamole into the tomato shells, dividing it evenly, then garnish with coriander leaves and pieces of tomato. Serve immediately.

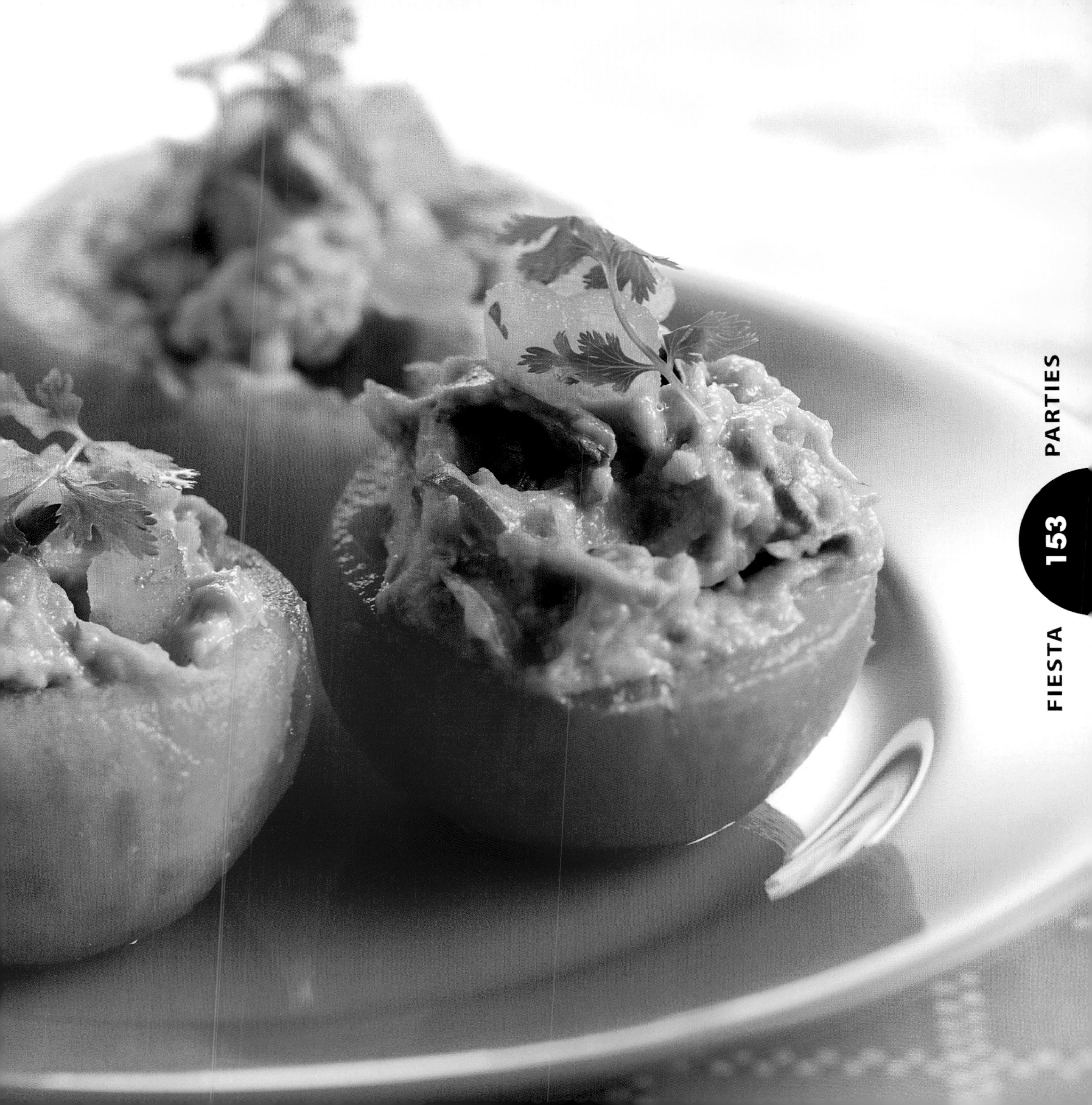

Masa de Tamales (receta básica)

Tamales Dough (basic recipe)

125g/4½oz softened butter or lard • 600g/1¼lb masa harina: see basic recipe (p. 8) • 750ml/1¼ pint/3 cups chicken stock • 2 tsp baking powder • 1 tsp salt

TAMALA FEASTS Apart from being sold in market stalls as snacks, *tamales* are also real party food. The parties at which these snacks are the centre of attention are even called *tamaladas*. There is always plenty of beer, wine, fruit juice and, of course, tequila, and the *tamales* are served with various salsas.

1 Beat the butter or lard in a bowl until it is light and creamy.
2 In another bowl, mix the masa harina with the stock, gradually adding the stock until a fairly firm dough is formed. Add the baking powder and salt and mix well.
3 Add the masa harina mixture slowly to the butter and beat until the mixture forms a smooth dough.
4 Check if the dough is ready by dropping a little bit of it in a bowl of cold water. When the dough floats, it is ready. Otherwise, you have to keep beating it for a little longer. Use as required.

Tamales con Pollo y Guindillas

Tamales with Chicken and Chillies

Tamales dough: see basic recipe (p.154) • 32 dried corn leaves, left whole or 15 banana leaves, halved • 1 tbsp corn oil • 2 fresh green Lombok chillies, chopped • 1 tbsp fresh oregano leaves, chopped • 1 clove garlic, crushed • 250g/ 9oz skinless boneless chicken, poached and chopped • 1 tbsp plain flour • 2 tomatoes, skinned and chopped • 1 tbsp almonds, toasted and chopped • 1 tbsp sesame seeds, toasted

1 Put the corn leaves in a bowl, pour over hot water and leave to soak for 30 minutes.
2 Heat the oil in a frying pan over a high heat, add the chillies, oregano and garlic and fry for 1 minute, stirring continuously.
3 Stir in the chicken, flour, tomatoes, almonds and sesame seeds and simmer until the mixture thickens, stirring continuously.
4 Drain the corn leaves and pat them dry with kitchen paper.
5 Take 2 tablespoons of tamales dough and flatten it, then put it on a corn leaf and place 1 tablespoon of chicken filling on top. Take 1 more tablespoon of tamales dough, flatten it again, then place it over the filling and seal around the edges, enclosing the filling completely.
6 Fold the corn leaf around the dough parcel, fold another corn leaf around it in the opposite direction and tie with kitchen string. Repeat with the other corn leaves, tamales dough and chicken filling until you have 15 tamales.
7 Bring a pan full of water to the boil. If you wish, you can line the steaming basket with the 2 remaining corn leaves, to protect the tamales against the steam. Do leave some space between the leaves. Put the tamales in the steamer, but not too close together, because the tamales expand slightly during steaming.
8 Place the steaming basket over the pan of boiling water and steam the tamales for 45-60 minutes or until they are completely cooked. The tamales are cooked when the corn leaf comes off easily. Check every now and then to make sure there is sufficient water in the pan and add more, if necessary. Serve the tamales hot.

Tamales con Filete de Lubina

Tamales with Wolffish Fillet

Tamales dough: see basic recipe (p. 154) • 32 dried corn leaves, left whole or 15 banana leaves, halved • 3 cloves garlic • 1 fresh Poblano chilli or 2 fresh green Lombok chillies, deseeded and chopped • 2 tbsp fresh oregano, chopped • 3 tbsp fresh coriander, chopped • finely grated zest and juice of 2 limes • 4 firm wolffish fillets, or hake fillet, cut into strips

1 Put the corn leaves in a bowl, pour over hot water and leave to soak for 30 minutes.
2 For the chilli paste, purée the garlic, chilli, oregano, coriander, lime zest and lime juice in a blender or food processor, until you get a smooth consistency.
3 Put the fish in a bowl and cover all over with the chilli paste. Leave to marinade for 2 hours in a cool place.
4 Place 2 corn leaves partially on top of each other after you have drained and patted them dry. Spoon 2 tablespoons of tamales dough over the leaves, flatten it, put some marinaded fish on top and cover with 1 more tablespoon of tamales dough, flattening it again and sealing around the edges to enclose the filling completely. Fold the corn leaves together to cover the filling and tie the parcel with kitchen string.
5 Repeat with the other corn leaves, tamales dough and marinaded fish until you have 15 tamales.
6 Steam the tamales for 45-60 minutes or until they are completely cooked (see p. 156). Serve the tamales hot.

TIP Corn leaves (or the best alternative: banana leaves) are not always available. The likeliest places you will find them are Indian supermarkets. If you really can't find them, non-stick baking paper is a fair alternative. It is a pity, because corn leaves do contain flavour, and this flavour is transferred to the filling during cooking. All the same, the fillings will taste excellent without them.
Another alternative would be to dry your own leaves: take the fresh leaves of an ear of corn, and dry them in an oven at 150°C/gas mark 2/300°F for about 30 minutes.

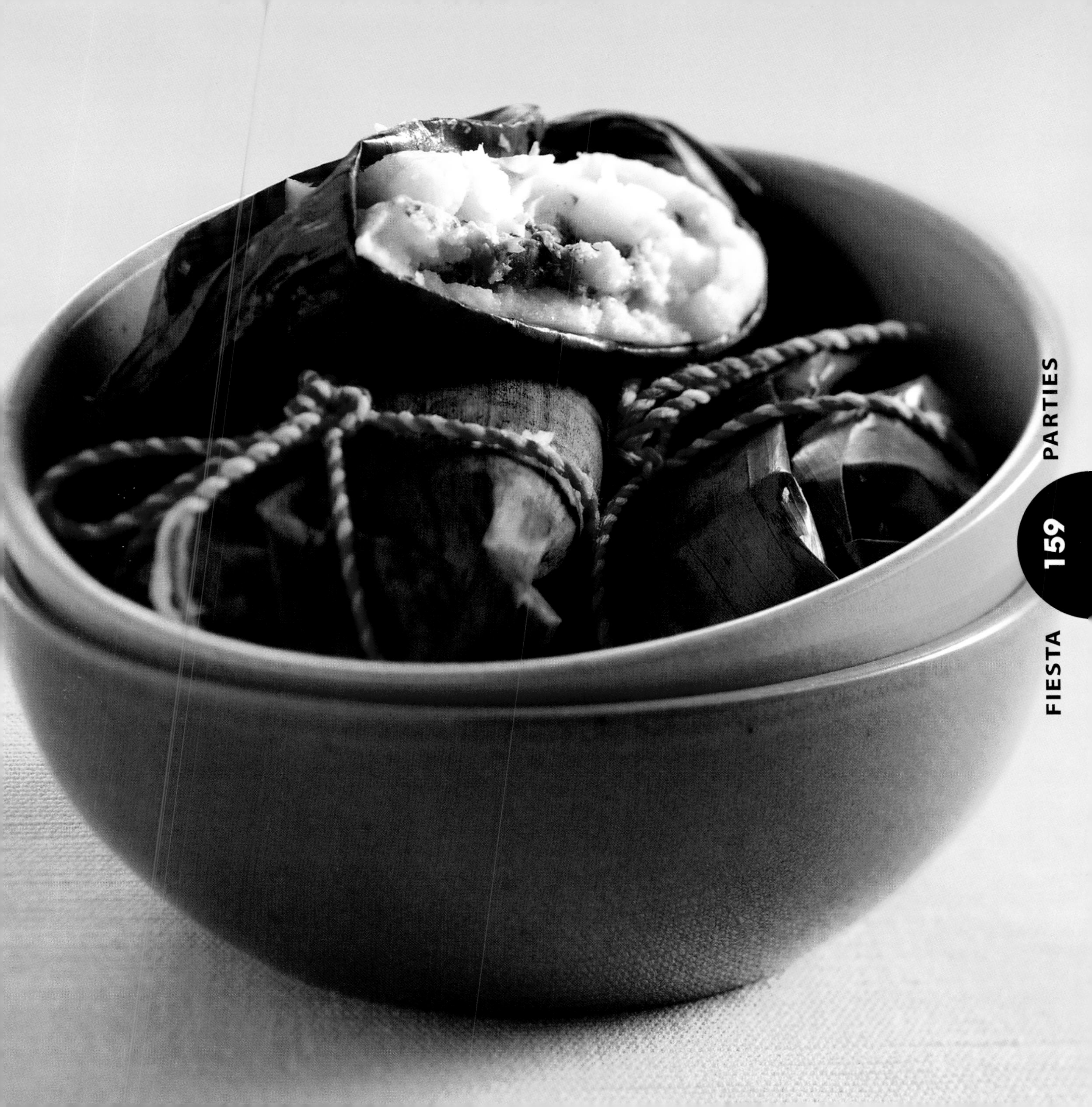

Tamales con Ananás y Coco

Tamales with Pineapple and Coconut

Tamales dough: see basic recipe (p. 154) • 32 dried corn leaves, left whole or 15 banana leaves, halved • 1 apple, peeled, cored and cut into pieces • 150g/5oz fresh or canned (prepared weight) pineapple, chopped • ½ fresh mango, peeled, stoned and chopped • 4 tbsp fresh coconut, grated • 1 tbsp pine nuts, toasted • 2 tbsp fresh mint, chopped

160

ALL SOULS' DAY One of the most important holidays during which eating, and especially tamales, play an important part, is the Day of the Dead. At the beginning of November the dead are remembered, and people believe that their souls will visit their specially decorated little altars. On these altars, people create a spread of all sorts of goodies, usually the favourite food of the person who is being commemorated. These little offerings are later eaten by the family, but the ghost of the deceased will still be floating around and enjoy the wonderful aromas of the dishes.

1 Put the corn leaves in a bowl, pour over hot water and leave to soak for 30 minutes. Drain the corn leaves and pat them dry with kitchen paper.
2 Meanwhile, for the filling, mix together the apple, pineapple, mango, coconut, pine nuts and mint in a bowl.
3 Take 2 tablespoons of tamales dough and flatten it. Put this on a corn leaf and put 1 tablespoon of the fruit filling on top. Take another 1 tablespoon of tamales dough, flatten it, then place it over the filling and seal around the edges, enclosing the filling completely.
4 Fold the corn leaf around the dough parcel, fold another corn leaf around it in the opposite direction, and tie with kitchen string. Repeat this with the other corn leaves, tamales dough and fruit filling until you have 15 tamales.
5 Steam the tamales for 45-60 minutes or until they are completely cooked (see p. 156). Serve hot.

Tamales Rellenos de Carne de Cerdo Picante

Tamales filled with Spicy Pork

Tamales dough: see basic recipe (p. 154) • 32 dried corn leaves, left whole or 15 banana leaves, halved • 500g/1¼lb lean pork, cut into in 5cm/2in cubes • 2 fresh Ancho chillies or 100g/4oz fresh red Lombok chillies • 1 clove garlic, finely chopped • 1 tbsp fresh oregano, chopped • 1 tbsp fresh coriander, chopped • 1 tbsp fresh thyme, chopped • ½ tsp ground cinnamon • ½ tsp black peppercorns, crushed • ½ tsp ground cumin • 1 tsp salt • 100ml/4fl oz/½ cup white wine vinegar • 3 tbsp corn oil

1   Put the corn leaves in a bowl, pour over hot water and leave to soak for 30 minutes. Drain the leaves and pat dry.
2   Meanwhile, place the pork in a large pan. Pour over enough water until it is covered. Bring to the boil, then lower the heat and simmer for 40 minutes.
3   Drain the pork. Save 100ml/4fl oz/½ cup of the cooking liquid and finely chop the meat. Set aside.
4   Meanwhile, roast the chillies in a dry frying pan for a few minutes until the skins are blackened. Cool briefly, then remove the skin and seeds, and chop the flesh into pieces. Put the chopped chillies in a bowl, pour hot water over the top and leave to soak for 15 minutes.
5   Strain the chillies (keep the liquid) and grind them to a paste in a blender or food processor, together with the garlic, oregano, coriander, thyme, cinnamon, peppercorns, cumin, salt and vinegar. If necessary, add 2 tablespoons of the reserved chilli liquid to make a sauce.
6   Heat the oil in a large pan, add the sauce and fry for 5 minutes. Add the pork and the reserved cooking liquid. Bring to the boil and boil until the liquid has evaporated. Leave the mixture to cool.
7   Take 2 tablespoons of tamales dough and flatten it. Put this on a corn leaf and put 1 tablespoon of the pork filling on top. Take another 1 tablespoon of tamales dough, flatten it again, then place it over the filling and seal around the edges, enclosing the filling completely.
8   Fold the corn leaf around the dough parcel, fold another corn leaf around it in the opposite direction, and tie with kitchen string. Repeat with the remaining corn leaves, tamales dough and pork filling until you have 15 tamales.
9   Steam the tamales for 45-60 minutes or until they are completely cooked (see p. 156). Put the hot tamales on a dish, and leave to stand for 10 minutes before serving.

Tamales con Guindilla y Pimiento

Tamales with Chillies and Peppers

Tamales dough: see basic recipe (p. 154) • 32 dried corn leaves, left whole or 15 banana leaves, halved • corn oil, for frying • 1 onion, coarsely chopped • 2 fresh Poblano chillies (or skinny fresh green Turkish chillies), roasted, skinned, deseeded and cut into strips • 2 small red peppers, roasted, skinned, deseeded and cut into strips • 4 cloves garlic, crushed • 50ml/2fl oz/¼ cup crème fraîche • 50ml/2fl oz/¼ cup beef stock • 50ml/2fl oz/¼ cup dry white wine • salt and freshly ground black pepper • 1 tbsp fresh thyme, chopped

1 Put the corn leaves in a bowl, pour over hot water and leave to soak for 30 minutes. Drain the leaves and pat dry.
2 Heat a little oil in a pan, add the onion and fry until golden brown. Add the chillies, peppers, garlic, crème fraîche, stock and white wine and leave to simmer until the liquid has almost completely evaporated. Season the mixture with salt, pepper and thyme. Remove the pan from the heat.
3 Take 2 tablespoons of tamales dough and flatten it. Put this on a corn leaf and put 1 tablespoon of the chilli filling on top. Take another 1 tablespoon of tamales dough, flatten it again, put it over the filling, and seal around the edges, enclosing the filling completely.
4 Fold the corn leaf around the dough parcel, fold another corn leaf around it in the opposite direction, and tie with kitchen string. Repeat with the remaining corn leaves, tamales dough and chilli filling until you have 15 tamales.
5 Steam the tamales for 45-60 minutes or until they are completely cooked (see p. 156). Serve hot.

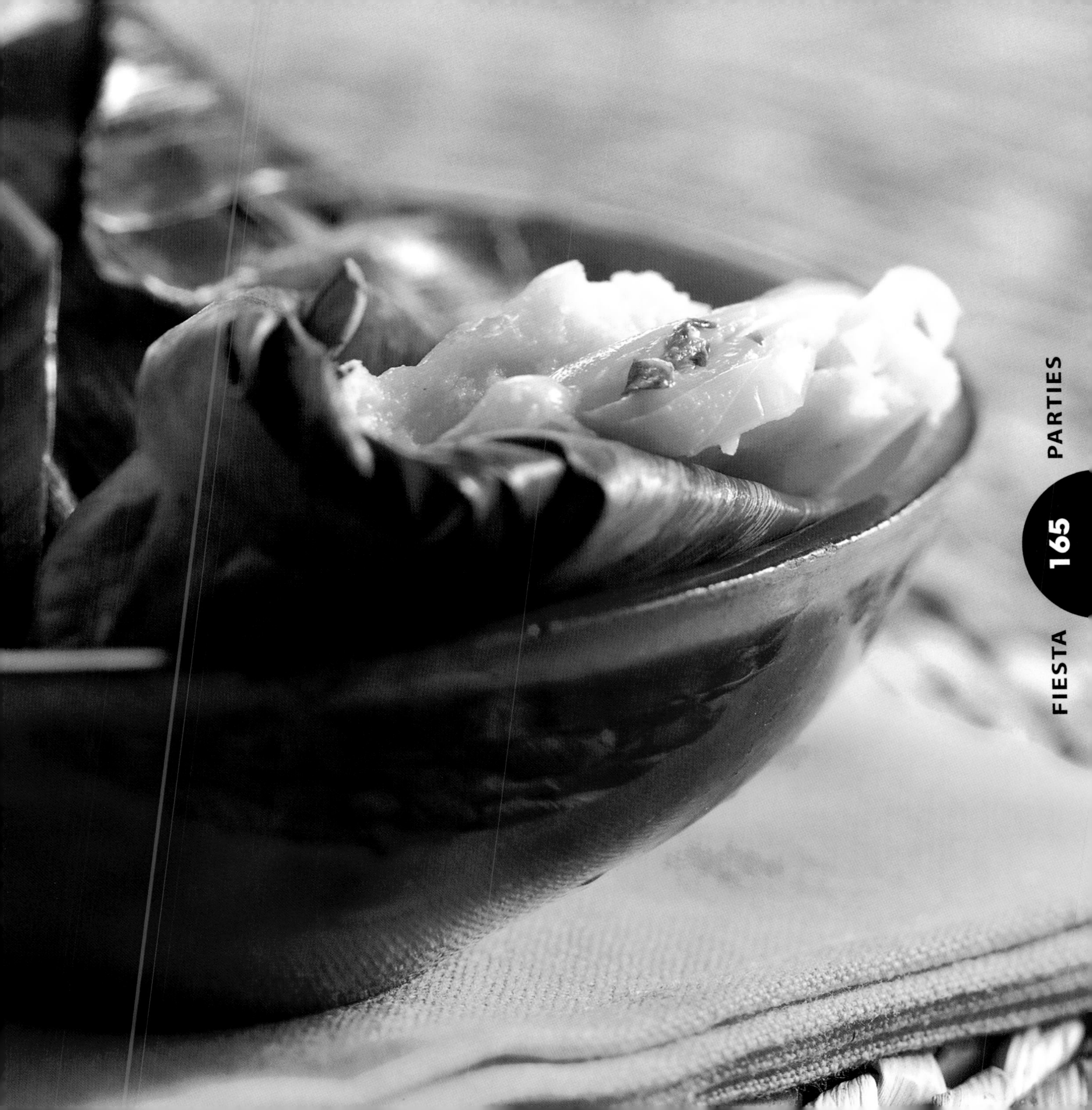

Tamales con Guindillas Pequeñas y Especias

Tamales with Chilli and Herbs

Tamales dough: see basic recipe (p. 154) • 32 dried corn leaves, left whole or 15 banana leaves, halved • 1½ tbsp corn oil • 1 onion, sliced • 2 cloves garlic, chopped • 4 fresh Poblano chillies, roasted, skinned, deseeded and cut into strips • 1½ tbsp crème fraîche • 2 tbsp fresh oregano, coarsely chopped • 2 tbsp fresh marjoram, coarsely chopped • 1 tbsp fresh flat-leaf parsley, coarsely chopped • salt, to taste

1 Put the corn leaves in a bowl, pour over hot water and leave to soak for 30 minutes. Drain the leaves and pat dry.
2 Heat the oil in a pan, add the onion and fry until golden brown. Add the garlic and chillies and fry for about 2 minutes.
3 Add the crème fraîche and leave to simmer until some of the liquid has evaporated. Season the mixture with oregano, marjoram, parsley and salt. Remove the pan from the heat.
4 Take 2 tablespoons of tamales dough, flatten it, place it on top of a corn leaf and spoon 1 tablespoon of chilli filling onto the dough. Take another 1 tablespoon of tamales dough, flatten it again, put it over the filling, and seal around the edges, enclosing the filling completely.
5 Fold the corn leaf around the dough parcel, fold another corn leaf around it in the opposite direction, and tie with kitchen string. Repeat with the remaining corn leaves, tamales dough and chilli filling, until you have 15 tamales.
6 Steam the tamales for 45-60 minutes or until they are completely cooked (see p. 156). Serve hot.

Tamales con Pasas

Tamales with Raisins

Tamales dough: see basic recipe (p. 154) • 32 dried corn leaves, left whole or 15 banana leaves, halved • 100g/4oz softened butter • 200ml/7fl oz/¾ cup milk • 4 ready-to-eat dried apricots, cut into pieces • 4 pitted dried dates, cut into pieces • 20g/¾oz raisins • 20g/¾oz pine nuts, toasted

TIP In Mexico, sweet and savoury tamales are served side by side at the table or the buffet. Originally, people also drank the milk or porridge-like *atole* to accompany them. Here it might be more fun to start the evening with savoury bites and close the evening with coffee and the sweet tamales. In that case, serve with traditional *café de olla*: a strong coffee, cooked in a large pan with brown sugar, cloves and cinnamon, which goes wonderfully with the sweet tamales.

1 Put the corn leaves in a bowl, pour over hot water and leave to soak for 30 minutes. Drain the leaves and pat dry.
2 Beat the butter in a bowl until light and fluffy. Add half of the milk and half of the tamales dough and beat well. Add the rest of the tamales dough, plus the remaining milk, a little at a time, until everything is mixed together well and the dough has the consistency of a thick cake dough. Set aside.
3 For the filling, mix the apricots, dates, raisins and pine nuts together in a bowl.
4 Take 2 tablespoons of the enriched tamales dough, flatten it, place it on top of a corn leaf and spoon 1 tablespoon of fruit filling onto the dough. Take another 1 tablespoon of tamales dough, flatten it again, put it over the filling, and seal around the edges, enclosing the filling completely.
5 Fold the corn leaf around the dough parcel, fold another corn leaf around it in the opposite direction, and tie with kitchen string. Repeat with the remaining corn leaves, tamales dough and fruit filling, until you have 15 tamales.
6 Steam the tamales for 45-60 minutes or until they are completely cooked (see p. 156). Serve hot.

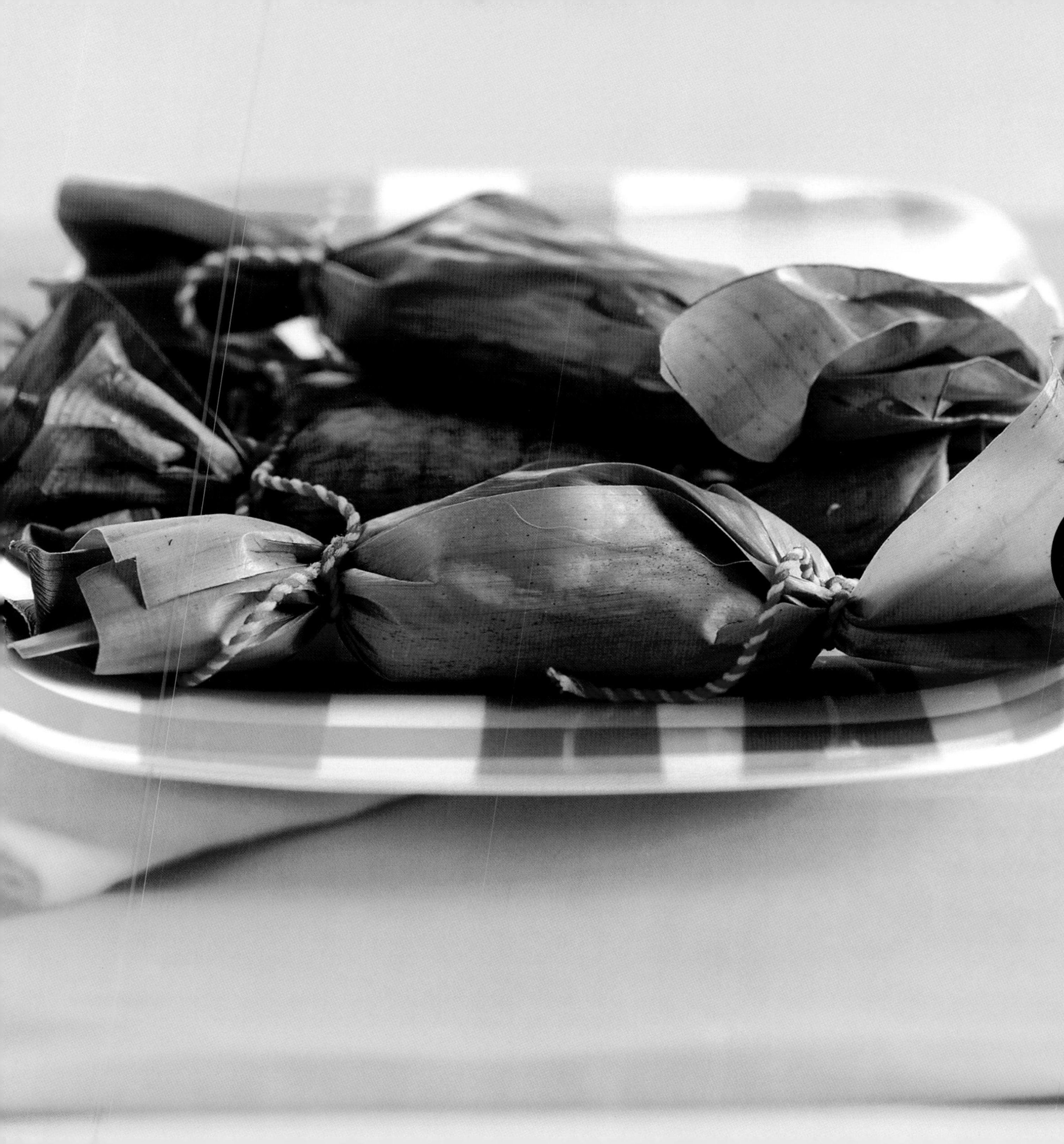

Tamales de Nuevo León

Tamales from Nuevo León

1 Put the corn leaves in a bowl, pour over hot water and leave to soak for 30 minutes. Drain and pat dry.
2 Bring 1 litre water to the boil in a pan, add the pork and salt and spoon off any scum that floats to the surface. Reduce the heat, cover the pan and leave the meat to simmer for about 40 minutes, until cooked.
3 Meanwhile, tear the chillies into flat pieces. Heat a frying pan, add a few pieces of chilli at a time, press them to the bottom of the pan with a spatula until they turn brown, then turn them and roast the other side in the same way. Repeat with the remaining chillies. Put the roasted chillies in a bowl. Pour over hot water and leave to soak for 20 minutes.
4 Pour the cooking liquid from the meat through a sieve, leave it to stand for a moment, then use a spoon to remove the fat from the surface. Place the meat on a plate and set aside.
5 Drain the chillies, then mix them with the peppercorns, cumin, garlic and 175ml/6fl oz/¾ cup pork stock. Blend to a liquid purée, then sieve it.
6 Heat the oil in a saucepan until the fat is really hot. Add the chilli purée and fry for 4-5 minutes, stirring regularly, until it becomes thicker and darker. Add 175ml/6fl oz/¾ cup pork stock, then leave the sauce to reduce on the heat for about 15 minutes, until you have about 100ml/4fl oz/½ cup left, stirring occasionally. Season with salt and the sugar.
7 Tear the meat into narrow strips and put these in a bowl. Mix the chilli sauce with the meat and raisins and leave to cool.
8 Place 2 tablespoons of tamales dough onto a corn leaf and flatten it. Spoon a heaped tablespoon of the meat mixture onto the dough. Take another 1 tablespoon of tamales dough, flatten it again, put it over the filling, and seal around the edges, enclosing the filling completely. Fold the two longer edges of the corn leaf together over the dough parcel and cover with the short edges. Tie the parcel with kitchen string. Repeat with the remaining corn leaves, tamales dough and pork filling until you have 15 tamales.
9 Steam the tamales for about 1 hour or until they are completely cooked (see p. 156). Leave to stand for 10 minutes before serving.

Tamales dough: see basic recipe (p. 154) • 15 dried corn leaves, left whole or 8 banana leaves, halved • 350g/12oz boneless pork shoulder, cut into 1cm cubes • 1 tbsp salt • 100g/4oz dried Lombok chillies, deseeded • 1 tsp black peppercorns, crushed • ½ tsp ground cumin • 1 large clove garlic, coarsely chopped • 1 tbsp corn oil • 1 tsp caster sugar • 2 tbsp raisins

Tamales de Maíz Fresco con Queso y Guindillas Picantes Tostadas

Fresh Corn Tamales with Cheese and Roast Chillies

Tamales dough: see basic recipe (p. 154) • 15 dried corn leaves, left whole or 8 banana leaves, halved • 2 fresh corn-on-the-cob or frozen or canned sweetcorn kernels (125-225g/4½oz-8oz) • 50g/2oz butter • salt • 1 fresh Poblano chilli or 2 fresh green Lombok chillies, roasted, deseeded and cut into strips • 200g/7oz fresh cheese, such as goat's cheese or feta cheese, cut into small pieces

1 Put the corn leaves in a bowl, pour over hot water and soak for 30 minutes. Drain the corn leaves and pat dry.
2 If using fresh corn-on-the-cob, use a sharp knife to cut the kernels off the cobs. Grind the fresh, frozen or canned sweetcorn kernels to a fine purée in a blender or food processor.
3 Place the corn purée in a bowl, add the tamales dough, butter and a little salt and mix together to form a thick paste.
4 Place 2 tablespoons of tamales dough mixture onto a corn leaf and flatten it. Place a piece of chilli and a little cheese over the dough, then put 1 more tablespoon of tamales dough over the top and flatten again. Seal around the edges, enclosing the filling completely. Fold the two longer edges of the corn leaf together over the dough parcel and cover with the short edges. Tie the parcel with kitchen string. Repeat with the remaining corn leaves, tamales dough mixture, chillies and cheese until you have 15 tamales.
5 Steam the tamales for about 1 hour or until they are completely cooked (see p. 156). Leave to stand for 10 minutes before serving.

Cheesecake con Almendras

Cheesecake with Almonds

160g/5½oz softened butter • 120g/4oz caster sugar • 6 eggs, separated • 400g/14oz quark • 500g/1¼lb mascarpone • finely grated zest of 4 oranges • 200g/7oz ground almonds • 150g/5oz self-raising flour, sifted • 300g/11oz white chocolate, chopped • one 26cm/10in springform/round cake tin, greased • icing sugar, for dusting

1 Preheat the oven to 180ºC/gas mark 4/350ºF. Beat the butter with the caster sugar in a bowl until pale and fluffy.
2 Whisk the egg yolks in a separate bowl, then stir them through the butter mixture together with the quark, mascarpone, orange zest, almonds and flour, mixing well.
3 In a separate bowl, whisk the egg whites until they are very stiff, then gently fold them through the orange mixture, together with the white chocolate.
4 Spoon the mixture into the prepared springform/cake tin and level the surface. Place the cheesecake in the centre of the oven. Bake for about 50 minutes (insert a skewer into the centre: if it comes out clean, the cheesecake is cooked).
5 Switch the oven off and leave the cheesecake to stand in the oven for another 15 minutes, with the door open.
6 Remove from the oven and let the cheesecake cool completely in the tin. Carefully unmould the cheesecake onto a serving plate, dust with sifted icing sugar, and serve cut into wedges.

Registro

INDEX

Conversion table

¼ teaspoon = 1.25ml
½ teaspoon = 2.5ml
1 teaspoon = 5ml

1 UK/US tablespoon = 15ml (3 tsp) = ½oz
1 Australian tablespoon = 20ml (4 tsp)

UK term	US term
Plain flour	All-purpose flour
Baking tray	Baking sheet
Courgette	Zucchini
Aubergine	Eggplant
Coriander	Cilantro
Cake tin	Cake/Baking pan
Maize flour	Cornmeal
Spring onions	Scallions
Rocket	Arugula
Pepper	Capsicum
Double cream	Heavy cream
Frying Pan	Skillet
Grill	Broiler
Caster sugar	Finely granulated sugar
Green pepper	Bell pepper
Icing sugar	Powdered sugar
Prawn	Small shrimp
Sweetcorn	Whole-kernel corn
Pudding	Dessert
Heaped spoonful	Heaping spoonful
Pastry	Pie crust
Ground rice	Rice flour
Stoned	Seeded
Frying pan	Skillet
Sieve	Strain, Strainer
(To) sift	(To) strain